CONTENTS

INTRODUCTION

'Walking is the best possible exercise.
Habituate yourself to walk very far.'

THOMAS JEFFERSON

Putting one foot in front of the other is one of the most natural of human activities. Most of us will, in the course of a day, do all sorts of walking – walking downstairs to breakfast in the morning, walking to the car, the bus stop or the railway station, walking to work or class, walking between offices and lecture theatres, popping down to the pub or the corner shop, taking your dog out – purposeful, yes, but borne of necessity.

This book is about walking, not for necessity, but for pleasure, enjoyment, satisfaction and happiness – a celebration of walking not because you're constrained to do it by the daily round but because you actually want to do it. We hope that this book will help you to appreciate walking for what it is – an infinitely rewarding pastime that will provide you with interest and enjoyment throughout your life.

In these pages you'll learn of:

- The benefits to you, and others, of walking (chapter 1)
- The history of walking for leisure (chapter 2)
- Getting started – basic and easy walking (chapter 3)
- How to get serious as a walker – wilder walking (chapter 4)
- The challenges of long-distance walking (chapter 5)
- Some remarkable and courageous – and very speedy – walkers (chapter 6)

So read on – but don't expect to finish the book. For hopefully within a few pages you'll have tightened your laces and be off down the road towards the nearest public footpath …

CHAPTER 1

WHY WALK?

'Walk and be happy, walk and be healthy.'
CHARLES DICKENS

*'The gym experience is not for everyone. Salvation
comes in the form of a good old-fashioned walk.'*
CLARE BALDING, TV PRESENTER

Walking is often called the perfect exercise. It's remarkable that something so simple can be so restorative, therapeutic and utterly rewarding in so many ways. In this section we look at why walking for enjoyment is great.

Walking is good for your health: The Ancient Greek physician Hippocrates described walking as 'man's best medicine'. In our day there's a wealth of scientific evidence to show that regular walking helps to reduce the risk of many diseases …

Stress
High blood pressure
Raised levels of cholesterol
Heart disease
Strokes
Some forms of cancer
Type 2 diabetes*

* Research by George Washington University suggests that a 15-minute walk after meals could help reduce the risk of contracting Type 2 diabetes.

… and enhances

Mood
Self-esteem

Here are some reported benefits from people who've come to enjoy walking through the *Walking For Health* organisation's Health Walk schemes:

- Feeling happy and energised
- Having more stamina
- Living longer, feeling fitter, enjoying life
- Keeping fit and independent in retirement
- Being able to enjoy life to the full
- Having a good, healthy heart, normal blood pressure and good circulation

Did you know that...
Recent research carried out at Harvard University found that walking for an hour a day increases life expectancy by four and a half years; even as little as 40 minutes' walking a week can increase life expectancy by nearly two years.

In the London borough of Tower Hamlets, a scheme called Walks On Prescription has been set up, where local GPs can refer patients for a 10-week walking programme – you may want to enquire of your GP if something similar exists in your area. Sustainable transport officer Rachel Maile explains that by joining the weekly walks, participants can 'proactively manage their weight, diabetes and other health conditions … and [are] encouraged to monitor their progress, week by week, towards a more active lifestyle.'

The Government, in recommending we all do at least 30 minutes of physical activity five times a week, suggests brisk walking as one form of activity. Studies show that people who choose to walk at least part of the way to work are more productive, happier and take less time off sick.

> **Did you know that...**
> *A 42 minute walk can walk off a pint of lager/ale*
> *A 56 minute walk can walk off a hot dog with white roll*
> *But it takes 2 hours 9 minutes to walk off a steak pie!*

Walking enhances creativity

Walking has been described as an all-round lift for the mind, body and soul, its regular rhythm helping creativity to blossom in the mind. Charles Dickens, the prolific nineteenth-century author, was a really keen walker and recorded in his diaries how he would go on 20-mile walks to conceive the plots of his novels. Louisa May Alcott was out walking when the idea for *Little Women*, one of the best-loved children's novels of all time, came to her, and she remembers that she could hardly wait to get home and start work on it. It was walking in the Malvern Hills in Worcestershire that inspired the great British composer Edward Elgar to write some of his most famous works, and those same hills gave similar inspiration to the novelist J. R. R. Tolkien and the poets William Langland and W. H. Auden. Charlotte Brontë clearly knew the value of a good walk; the first ten words of her novel *Jane Eyre*, one of the greatest novels of all time, express the eponymous heroine's regret that 'There was no possibility of taking a walk that day.' In the modern age, walking helps you escape the computer screen and gives you space to think through new projects.

Did you know that...
In April 1988 the English Test cricketer Ian Botham re-enacted the exploits of Hannibal and walked 500 miles (800 km) from Perpignan to Turin across the Alps with a troop of elephants, all in aid of leukaemia research.

Walking enhances your social life

The author, Mark Twain, wrote that 'the true charm of pedestrianism does not lie in the walking, or in the scenery, but in the talking.' Many people, among them BBC sports presenter Clare Balding, enjoy walking as a social activity. The popularity of walkers' clubs, which will be explored further later in this book, shows that there is something special and fulfilling in sharing a walking experience with someone else and making new friends as a result of a common interest in walking.

Walking can help others

Charity walking has increased massively in popularity in recent years. Many people, wanting to raise money for a worthy cause, have opted for sponsored walks, asking family and friends to pledge a certain sum for every mile walked or on successful completion. There's no reason why you can't organise your own. Some charities now organise specific events, bringing together large numbers of people to take on a walking challenge and asking the entrants to seek sponsorship. The British Heart Foundation, for example, now organises a London to Brighton trek consisting of a non-stop walk of 62 miles (100 km).

Other recent charity challenges with an individual twist include:

- A trek across Exmoor called the 30-30, walking 30 km (18.75 miles) or 30 miles (48 km) while carrying a pack weighing 30 lbs (13.5 kg)
- A walk of 62 miles (100 km) along the Thames Path by night
- A London Moon Walk consisting of a marathon length (26.2 miles or 42 km) walk starting at midnight with walkers wearing a decorated bra in support of Breast Cancer UK
- An annual 'Hike in Heels' organised by a hospice support group in Chichester, West Sussex, where men take to the streets in stilettos.

Many of the 'ultimate' walks, described later in this book, have been undertaken in order to raise money for charity. For instance, John Merrill's walk round the entire coastline of Great Britain, accomplished in 1978, raised more than £40,000 for the Royal Commonwealth Society for the Blind.

Walking is educational

Even a short walk can give you a valuable history or geography lesson or tell you about the wildlife and plant life in the locality. Walking gives you the time to take things in and enjoy them, unlike a journey by car, bus or train, where the scenery can whizz past without your appreciating any of it. Despite modern building and road development, which have lost us so many acres of precious countryside and historic landmarks, just walking a mile from your doorstep, whether in an urban or rural environment, will almost certainly put you in touch with the past, some interesting or picturesque geographical phenomenon, or an area of grassland or woodland which supports a variety of plants, insects or even animals. We may even find sources of food such as edible fungi, flora and seaweed, not to mention the ever-popular blackberry (going out blackberry picking is a great reason for walking in September!). We are blessed in Great Britain with a massive number of historic churches;

it's likely that there will be one such church just a short walk from you and whatever your religious inclination, entering and exploring the church will kindle your spirit and provide you a fascinating insight into community life, past and present.

Even just looking up as you walk can be an education in itself. Although our unpredictable British weather can be a nuisance, it provides an endless variety of cloudscapes. The wonderful book by Gavin Pretor-Pinney, *The Cloudspotter's Guide*, is great for explaining the difference between types of clouds, for example between the rippling mackerel cirrocumulus skies and the nimbostratus, promising rain. You can become a weather forecaster just by walking!

And, of course, having tasted the educational value of a short walk from your doorstep, you may want to spread your wings and go further afield, perhaps travelling by car, bus or train to savour the historic, architectural, geographical or wildlife highlights of other areas, or joining an organised city or wildlife walk.

Walking is an adventure

There's something romantic and intimate about travelling on foot. In no other means of transport are you closer to what's actually going on around you. What's more, you're not dependent on a vehicle – you are entirely dependent on yourself and your ability to propel yourself.

> *'"What none of you young fellows appear to realise," I said, "is that Clarice Fitch is essentially a romantic girl. The fact that she crosses Africa on foot, when it would be both quicker and cheaper to take a train, proves this."'*
>
> P. G. WODEHOUSE, *THERE'S ALWAYS GOLF*

Did you know that...
In 2010, Ed Stafford became the first man to walk the entire length of the Amazon; his two and a half year journey saw him confronting alligators, jaguars, pit vipers and machete-wielding tribesmen.

Many famous figures, who have distinguished themselves principally in other fields, have embarked on walking adventures during their lives.

Laurie Lee

Laurie Lee was born in 1914 and died in 1997. Setting out in 1934 from his Cotswold home, Lee walked first to London then sailed to Spain, walking across that country from north to south and scraping a living by playing his violin outside street cafes. His adventure is recounted in his 1969 book *As I Walked Out One Midsummer Morning*.

Having completed his walk through Spain, he volunteered in the Spanish Civil War but his service was cut short by epilepsy and he returned to England. Lee became a journalist and scriptwriter and during World War Two he made documentary films and became publications editor for the Ministry of Information. It was in 1959 that he published the work for which he became most famous, *Cider With Rosie*, about his childhood in Slad, Gloucestershire, where he returned in later life. It took him two years and three drafts to complete the memoir.

> *'I was tasting the extravagant quality of being free.'*
> LAURIE LEE, *AS I WALKED OUT ONE MIDSUMMER MORNING*

> *'I followed this straight southern track for several days…
> There was really no hurry. I was going nowhere.'*
> LAURIE LEE, *AS I WALKED OUT ONE MIDSUMMER MORNING*

'All horsepower corrupts.'
PATRICK LEIGH FERMOR

Eric Newby

Eric Newby was born in 1919 and died in 2006. His taste for adventure was demonstrated when he was just 19 by a sea voyage from Australia to Europe via Cape Horn. He was awarded the Military Cross for his part in the Allied raid on Sicily in August 1942. His book, *A Short Walk In The Hindu Kush*, was the written account of his adventure in the Nuristan mountains of Afghanistan, and was described by the American novelist Rick Skwiot as being told with 'understatement, self-effacement, savage wit, honed irony and unrelenting honesty.' In 1963 he was made travel editor for the *Observer* newspaper and was subsequently given a Lifetime Achievement Award of the British Guild of Travel Writers.

Patrick Leigh Fermor

Patrick Leigh Fermor was born in 1915 and died in 2011. He was just 18 when he decided to walk across Europe from Hook of Holland to Constantinople, arriving at his destination two years later. He took with him little more than a few clothes, letters of introduction, and some books of poetry. He slept in barns and shepherds' huts but was also invited into many country houses owned by the aristocracy. His adventures are recounted in *A Time of Gifts, Between the Woods and the Water* and *The Broken Road*. Fermor then spent some years travelling about the more remote parts of Greece on foot and by mule. During World War Two he belonged to the Special Operations Executive, playing a prominent part in the Cretan Resistance. He was described by a BBC journalist as a 'cross between Indiana Jones, James Bond and Graham Greene.' He was knighted in 2004 having previously received the DSO and OBE.

Walking gives you access all areas

Not quite all, but moving in that direction. Later in the book we'll look at the wonder that is CROW (Countryside and Rights of Way Act 2000) – a piece of legislation that gives walkers in many parts of the country the right to go wherever they like. But even where the 'right to roam' is restricted, walkers can reach parts of the countryside that are quite inaccessible to motorists or even cyclists or horse-riders.

'I am monarch of all I survey; my right there is none to dispute.'
WILLIAM COWPER

*'Roadside verges always stink of petrol fumes, whereas
two hundred yards away over the stile it is possible
to smell the wild fragrance of the countryside.'*
H. D. WESTACOTT, *THE WALKER'S HANDBOOK*

It's true that many roads, even major roads, can take the motor traveller through magnificent scenery, but by their very nature they cannot provide a pollution-free countryside experience. And while many footpaths can and are used by cyclists, a very great number of them are for walkers only – where walkers alone can savour a remoteness and peace, uncluttered by reminders of the modern, ephemeral and temporal world. Moreover, through punishing terrain the cyclist will always be mindful of the potential damage to his or her machine and the possibility of mechanical breakdown. A walker has none of these concerns and can enjoy a variety of scenic experiences that is unparalleled by any other form of transport. Arguably the best is a hilltop. There is something particularly special about walking to a summit and gazing down on the landscape below which may be rural, a seemingly endless patchwork of fields, dotted with villages and farmsteads, or may provide a bird's eye view of one of our great cities. The good news is that you don't need to have the mountaineering skills of Sir Edmund Hillary and you don't require ice axes or crampons to appreciate the beauty of the British landscape.

Six experiences for walkers only!

- *A ridgetop march in a Cumbrian mountain range*
- *Climbing to the highest point in England (Scafell Pike, Cumbria)*
- *A coastal walk over the cliffs of Cornwall*
- *A beachcombing walk*
- *Bogtrotting across Dartmoor*
- *A woodland walk on Exmoor*

Each one brings its own atmosphere, surroundings, colours, aromas, and joys – just for the walker.

'The whole object of travel is not to set foot on foreign land – it is at last to set foot on one's own country as a foreign land.'

G. K. CHESTERTON

Walking is fulfilling

Later in this book you will read of some walkers who have achieved great things, from walking the coastline of Great Britain to walking right round the world. Their motives will have varied, but they did it, at least in part, because they wanted to tell themselves they could. In the same way, whether you walk for others or for yourself, you can learn much about yourself, your inner strength, your self-discipline and resolve, through walking, whether because of the nature of terrain, the distance you're covering or in conquering any physical or psychological fears you may have.

Alfred Wainwright, whom we'll meet again later in this book, wrote of conquering the Pennine Way, one of the biggest walking challenges in Britain:

> *'You do it because you want to prove to yourself that you are man enough to do it. You do it because you count it a personal achievement. Which it is, precisely. You will be more ready to tackle other big ventures and more able to bring them to a successful conclusion.'*
>
> A. WAINWRIGHT, *PENNINE WAY COMPANION*

If you think just 'walking' is unproductive or unable to stir the soul, you could always be doing something else at the same time. Here are just a few wacky walking records set recently...

 Emily Miethner threw and caught an apple sixty times when walking forward in an apple orchard in Lancaster, Massachusetts, in September 2012

 Rolf Iven holds the record for the longest distance walked on hot plates, namely 75 ft 1 inch (22.9 metres) in Milan, in April 2009

 Montystar Agarwal lifted a 50 lb (22.65 kg) weight with his hair and walked 12 metres (13 yds) at Goa Arijuna in November 2012

 Patrick Young walked on his hands for 1 minute 10.22 seconds at Lewisville, Texas in February 2013

 Mariappan Palanichamy lifted a 40 lbs (18 kg) weight using just his mouth and walked 50 metres (54 yds) at Dindigul, Tamil Nadu in February 2013

 Doug McManaman walked 2,000 yards (1.8 km) while balancing an egg on the back of his hand in Cumberland County, Novia Scotia in July 2013

 Tai Star walked 10 metres (11 yds) on a barrel in 29.8 seconds in Tucson, Arizona in April 2013

And the great news is, walking needn't cost anything

In difficult economic times, walking is particularly brilliant because it is free. If you're starting your walk from home, the only financial outlay required for the walking itself is a weatherproof coat and some comfortable shoes – but you may have those already. It is true that if you go on a guided walk there may be a fee to pay or the expectation of a gratuity to your leader at the end, but if you go walking independently, whether on your own, or with companions, it will cost you nothing. Unlike many outdoor activities, you need no special training or tuition (although later in the book we'll look at what you *will* need in order to develop as a walker). You can start now! You do not need the fitness and stamina levels required for running or other energetic sports such as football or tennis. You can continue to enjoy it at any age. Once you start walking, it is only tiredness in your legs or feet that will compel you to stop. The body has a remarkable ability to keep going and support you no matter how far you choose to walk.

Now let's see how it all started…

THE DEVELOPMENT OF WALKING FOR ENJOYMENT

'Away we went in jubilant mood, determined to carry out the assault on Kinder Scout.'

BENNY ROTHMAN'S MEMORIES OF THE KINDER TRESPASS AS QUOTED IN SINCLAIR MCKAY'S BOOK *RAMBLE ON*

It may seem incongruous that in an age obsessed by technology and other sophisticated forms of entertainment, the simple pastime of walking is so popular. And even more incongruously, perhaps, it is only in the comparatively recent past that walking for pleasure has become the boom industry that it undoubtedly now is.

Walking becomes fun

Paths have been with us since prehistoric times, but not for leisure reasons. They were established for trading purposes and linked centres where essentials of prehistoric life were to be found. A classic example of a prehistoric trading route is the Great Ridgeway which linked Lyme Regis in Dorset with Hunstanton in Norfolk, the route serving as a drove road, a trading route, and a convenient track for invaders. Though some routes, previously trading routes, were used by pilgrims, e.g. between Winchester and Canterbury, these paths were never intended, or used, for enjoyment. During the Middle Ages paths became used as a means of getting about the countryside by the shortest route. Although people might enjoy a stroll around a park or garden for leisure, or 'take the air' for health reasons, as recently as the eighteenth century rambling for pleasure was virtually unheard of in Britain. In 1782 a German pastor, Carl Moritz, commented that the pedestrian in Britain seems to be 'considered as a sort of wild man or an out-of-the-way being who is stared at, pitied, suspected and shunned by everybody who meets him.'

Did you know that...
A survey conducted by the walkers' organisation Ramblers revealed that 77 per cent of adults in the UK, equating to roughly 38 million people, walk for pleasure at least once a month, and nearly two thirds of these cover an excess of two miles at a time. It's estimated that 18 million Britons enjoy regular country walks.

It was only towards the end of the eighteenth and into the nineteenth century that paths began to be used for recreational purposes, a welcome relief from polluted environments and the strains of daily life brought about by the Industrial Revolution. The novels of Thomas Hardy and Jane Austen have many references to recreational walks on public paths. The poet William Wordsworth and his contemporary, Samuel Taylor Coleridge, were both keen walkers; the essayist William Hazlitt walked with Coleridge and although he claimed he couldn't see the virtue of walking and talking at the same time he wrote: 'Give me the blue sky over my head, and the green turf beneath my feet, a winding road before me, and three hours' march to dinner… '

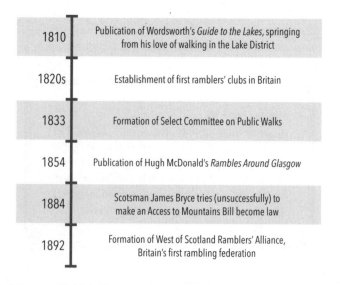

1810	Publication of Wordsworth's *Guide to the Lakes*, springing from his love of walking in the Lake District
1820s	Establishment of first ramblers' clubs in Britain
1833	Formation of Select Committee on Public Walks
1854	Publication of Hugh McDonald's *Rambles Around Glasgow*
1884	Scotsman James Bryce tries (unsuccessfully) to make an Access to Mountains Bill become law
1892	Formation of West of Scotland Ramblers' Alliance, Britain's first rambling federation

Did you know that...
It's estimated that Wordsworth had walked some 180,000 miles (288,000 km) by the age of sixty-five.

Did you know that...
The first walk from Land's End to John o'Groats was undertaken in September 1871 by Robert and John Naylor, wealthy brothers from Cheshire. They were inspired to do the end to end walk by reading literature about walks to Land's End from London and to John o'Groats from London.

It took them eight days just to get to the start, as they began by sailing to the Shetlands, sailing from there to Thurso and walking from Thurso to the start. They said they did this to avoid repeating anything! Displaying very impressive levels of fitness, they averaged 25 miles a day and their complete end-to-end walk was 1,372 miles (2,195 km) in length. They never walked on Sundays. It took them nine weeks to complete the journey.

During the nineteenth century rambling clubs continued to be established in northern England and the popularity of rambling was still growing in the early years of the twentieth century. During the inter-war years thousands of unemployed people left the industrial cities of the north every weekend, walking the hills of Derbyshire, Northumberland and Yorkshire. By the early 1930s, a number of walkers' federations had been formed and in 1931 six regional federations representing walkers from across Britain created the National Council of Ramblers' Federations. The walking movement was gaining momentum!

But – and it was a big but – the interests of walkers were still in fierce competition with private landowners closing off their land and refusing public access to it. The huge network of signed and mapped footpaths and bridleways we enjoy today simply didn't exist. Walkers at that time wanted more, much more access. Landowners dug in their heels.

The battle lines were drawn…

The Kinder Trespass

One of the most popular areas for recreational walking at this time was the Peak District in Derbyshire. From the late 1890s climbers were turning their attention to the gritstone edges of the northern part of the Peak District, the so-called Dark Peak area, with bog-trotting – the traversing of tough sections of moorland – proving increasingly popular. By the 1930s some weekends saw as many as 10,000 walkers in the area. However, walkers found themselves frustrated at the lack of access to large parts of the moor. On 24 April 1932 around five hundred walkers decided to make a stand against this. They assembled at the small town of Hayfield, a gateway to the Dark Peak, and set off into prohibited territory in peaceful protest. A group of gamekeepers met them, fighting broke out, the police intervened and as a result, a number were prosecuted and five spent time in prison. But their efforts were not in vain. The protestors excited massive support and sympathy from those who wanted greater access to our wonderful countryside.

The Ramblers

It was less than three years after the Kinder Trespass that the Ramblers Association (later the Ramblers) was founded to represent the interests of recreational walkers at national level.

Things you may not know about the Ramblers

Every year, its volunteers
lead 28,000 group
walks attracting over
half a million ramblers

It was instrumental in the
establishment of National
Parks and National Trails

Throughout its existence
the Ramblers Association
has campaigned for
increased access to
the countryside

It was officially created
on 1 January 1935

In 2013, its president was the well-known TV presenter Julia Bradbury

In recent years they have been campaigning for the preservation and safeguarding of the National Trails, the official long-distance footpaths, in Britain

In 2007, they launched a Get Walking, Keep Walking project in England aimed at helping inactive people in the inner cities to walk independently through a 12-week walking programme. This project received a lottery grant and is estimated to have helped over 100,000 people

The Ramblers have campaigned robustly to secure public access to the coast in Wales and England, and in May 2012 achieved a notable victory with the opening of the complete Wales Coastal Path. They have called on the Government to go further and create a path round the whole coastline of England as well.

National Parks

The concept of National Parks sounds modern but the first National Park in the world, Yellowstone in the USA, was established in 1872. It was 'dedicated and set apart as a public park or pleasuring ground for the benefit and enjoyment of the people.' Years before that, William Wordsworth had a similar vision for his beloved Lake District. Numerous Bills were laid before the British Parliament during the early part of the twentieth century to improve public access to areas of outstanding beauty, but none were successful. It was only during the Second World War that an architect, John Dower, was commissioned to write a report with a view to the establishment of National Parks, which in 1942 were stated to be long overdue. John Dower defined a National Park in this way:

'An extensive area of beautiful and relatively wild country in which…
The characteristic landscape beauty is strictly preserved
Access and facilities for public open air enjoyment (are) amply provided
Wildlife and places of architectural and historic interest (are) suitably protected
Established farming use is effectively maintained.'

During World War Two a blueprint for National Parks and greater access to the countryside was laid down and these were realised by the most important piece of legislation for recreational walkers ever enacted:

The National Parks and Access to Countryside Act 1949.
   This Act proposed:

- Setting up of a National Parks Commission
- A framework for defining rights of way
- Access agreements with landowners to give free access to open country
- The establishment of long distance footpaths

The 1949 Act provided a legislative framework for establishing the National Parks. Twelve areas in the United Kingdom were proposed for National Park status and all subsequently achieved it, ten of them during the 1950s. The ownership of the land didn't change: for each an executive committee was appointed, responsible for regulating development within the National Park and providing amenities for visitors.

National Parks have proved one of the great success stories in the history of walking for pleasure. Assisted by tight controls on development, preserving rights of access, protection of wildlife and habitats, and characterised by immense beauty and the individual character of each one, the concept of the National Park is still thriving today. They provide some of the best opportunities for challenging and rewarding walking in Great Britain. We'll look at them in greater detail in chapter 4.

Access to the countryside

The 1949 Act laid upon local authorities a statutory duty to compile and publish Definitive Maps showing all public paths on a scale not less than 1:25,000 (the scale of the Ordnance Survey Explorer Maps). Where there was a dispute as to whether a path was a public right of way or not, the first resort was negotiation and, if that failed to resolve the issue, there would be a public inquiry and a final decision would be taken by the Minister of Town and Country Planning. The importance of the Definitive Map was huge, because it conclusively proved that something shown as a right of way was a right of way – even if it was included by mistake! – and legislation ensured that the local authority had the duty to keep it open, only diverting or extinguishing it by due legal process, and landowners had to ensure that its course remained (and remains) unobstructed.

The law also allows for new paths to be created, but the authorities responsible for authorising such a path must bear in mind the effect on the rights of those interested in the land. The number of creation orders is small. There are also so-called permissive paths which aren't public footpaths as such but where the landowner allows the public to use a path subject to his right to impose limitations and withdraw permission in certain circumstances.

Although this all sounds good news to walkers, the Ramblers wanted more – the so-called right to roam in England and Wales.

> **Did you know that...**
> *There are about 100,000 miles (160,000 km) of public paths in England and Wales.*

The right to roam

This was the right to unhindered access to open country – although not, obviously, private property or cultivated land. Despite the proposal in the 1949 Act of arrangements for 'free access', ramblers had to wait until the Countryside and Rights of Way Act 2000 (known as CROW) for the implementation of rights to roam in open country in England and Wales. Not that this Act provided unlimited rights. The Act provided that they be implemented region by region and not all uncultivated land was covered by the legislation.

Right to roam Q & A

Q. What might be considered open/uncultivated country?
A. Moorland
   Mountains
   Heathland
   Downland
   Woodland
   The coast

In Scotland this right was already available. So, for instance, if before the year 2000 you wanted to walk the coastline of Great Britain, you'd be able to walk as near as you liked to the shoreline in Scotland, but you'd be forced to use the nearest right of way to the coast in England and Wales. This meant you'd often have to stay some way back from the shoreline. Although the 'right to roam' was available in Scotland even before 2000, it was given statutory recognition by the Land Reform (Scotland) Act 2003, confirming unhindered access to open country in Scotland.

Right to roam Q & A

Q. So how do you know where you can roam?
A. As each particular piece of open country acquired
the right to roam provision it was designated
as 'access land' and shown as such on the larger
scale Ordnance Survey maps. The newer Explorer
maps show where access land can be found, using
a distinctive brown-shaded boundary. Woodlands
are marked with either a pale green for access
land or a darker shade of green for areas not
designated as access land.

The significance of 'access land' is huge. It means that while you're in the access land, you're not restricted to public footpaths. You can walk anywhere!

Of course, the right to roam is subject to obvious restrictions such as non-interference with important countryside activity (such as farming), not endangering the life of the countryside, and following the Countryside Code which is set out in chapter 3.

Long-distance paths

The vision of the 1949 Act for long-distance footpaths became a reality. The first to open was the Pennine Way in 1965. The Pennine Way was the brainchild of Tom Stephenson, sometime secretary of the Ramblers Association, who by what John Hillaby described as 'dogged bargaining, barter and compromise' negotiated with landowners to create a continuous right of way across the Pennines – the southern end of which crossed the very land into which the Kinder Trespassers had dared to enter back in 1932. A further eighteen officially designated long-distance routes now exist in Great Britain, together with a vast number of 'named' long-distance paths. For more information on long-distance walking routes, see chapter 5.

Nowadays walking for pleasure is thriving. Just a glance at the Internet will show you how many walkers' clubs there are; most towns now boast at least one shop specialising in the sale of outdoor goods for walkers; there are several magazines devoted to walking for pleasure; and Julia Bradbury's *Railway Walks* and *Wainwright Walks* are shown frequently on national television.

Walking has never been more popular and never been easier to take up seriously.

So now it's your turn…

CHAPTER 3

GETTING STARTED – EASY WALKING FOR PLEASURE

'Travelling on foot can be meditative, fostering a slow frame of mind.'
CARL HONORÉ, *IN PRAISE OF SLOW*

Walking for pleasure isn't like learning a musical instrument or a sport. It is literally possible to start by putting down this book (or whatever else you happen to be doing) and setting off. It really is that easy.

That said, if you're to enjoy walking, it's important that you aren't put off by things going wrong during your first few walks for pleasure, whether they're a retirement hobby or a regular post Sunday lunch stroll.

Walkers' Woes

You get lost • You get wet or muddy • You get too hot or too cold • You get thirsty or hungry • You wear yourself out • You get sore feet or blisters

---

You can avoid all these common afflictions if you plan a little and think a little – and indeed all of the avoidance techniques set out below hold good for all your walking for pleasure in future.

Are those weather sayings true?

Red sky at night, shepherd's delight – *if the cause of the red sky is rays of the setting sun reflected on very high clouds, it means a cold front has passed and settled weather is on the way*

Red sky in the morning, shepherd's warning – *if the cause of the red sky is the rays of the morning sun shining on high clouds, it means a warm front is approaching, bringing rain*

Rain before seven, fair before eleven – *unless the depression bringing the rain is very deep, evidenced by very thick fast-moving low-lying clouds, it rarely rains non-stop for more than four hours*

Be prepared

Avoid getting lost...

... by basing your initial walks from your home where you'll be familiar with the local area, and sticking to the roads, paths and tracks you know. There'll be plenty of time to be more adventurous once you've  got more experienced. Using familiar walkways obviates the need to read a map and avoids any risk of trespass. You'll appreciate the surroundings more as well. If you live or are staying in a seaside town, you'll be hugely blessed, as you can follow the promenade or the beach (being careful to watch the tide!); again, good easy walking that poses no navigational difficulty, and with the bonus of the sights of the sea and good sea air. Similarly, there may be areas of woodland in your area with well marked and firm forest trails. If you're able to read a map there's no reason why you can't be more adventurous, but early on it's better to stick with what you know, and as your map reading skills improve (see chapter 4) you can become a little bolder!

Another way to avoid getting lost is to go out with companions who know the way, or on a guided walk. To find out what guided walks are on offer in your locality, just check with your nearest tourist information office. Walking organisations as a means of getting into more ambitious walking are discussed at the end of the chapter.

Avoid getting wet...

... by making sure you go walking when it's dry and forecast to stay that way for however long you're out. While long-range  forecasting is notoriously inaccurate, short-range forecasts, especially those given on the BBC, are generally very reliable and experience indicates that it's very rare indeed for it to rain following a forecast of dry weather. Walking in the rain can be fun, but getting wet through is no fun at all. Of course, if you're going out on a longer, 'serious' walk, where rain is likely to affect you, there are ways you can protect yourself from wet weather, but if you're a beginner, just don't go out in the rain. Unless you're sticking to pavements and there's no wind, it's not a good idea to go out walking with an umbrella. As far as muddying your clothes is concerned, it's best in the early days to avoid paths prone to mud, but if that's not possible, pop on some overtrousers or wellies (although wellies aren't to be recommended for walks of more than half a day).

Avoid getting too hot or too cold...

... by wearing appropriate clothing. The best advice here, which is equally valid for more adventurous walking, is to wear thin clothing which you can add to or subtract by extra or fewer layers depending on how hot or cold you are. The layers should be capable of covering the arms and the legs if the sun is hot. That may seem incongruous but unprotected skin exposed to hot sun will almost certainly get burnt. In particularly hot sunshine a sun hat is advisable. Excessive cold is equally unpleasant, if not more so, so add more layers including gloves if necessary, and a woolly hat which will cover the ears. Cold ears can be very uncomfortable! You can always take off outer layers once you've worked up some heat.

Avoid thirst...

... by taking a bottle of water and drinking from it at frequent regular intervals and not waiting until you're thirsty. Thirst is the consequence of dehydration and by then it's too late. Thirst is a hidden menace – it's impossible to imagine how bad it is until you're experiencing it for yourself, and when you do, you're unable to think of anything else except quenching it. By drinking regularly and frequently from the start, you'll avoid thirst on even the hottest days. Of course, as well as your trusty water bottle, another tip – and indeed one of the great joys when walking – is to factor in a visit to a pub or cafe where you can refresh yourself with a drink of tea, coffee or something stronger. Similarly, you can avoid hunger by taking food with you; you may not need much on a short walk, especially on top of Sunday lunch, but a couple of hours' brisk walking soon builds up an appetite. You may want to invest in a small rucksack to avoid having to carry your food or drink in a bag or a pocket. When you embark on longer walks, it becomes essential that you do have proper supplies of food and drink.

Avoid wearing yourself out...

... by making sure you aren't over-ambitious. It's a bad idea to walk five miles from home and then realise your legs and feet are so stiff and achey you can't actually walk home again, especially if you've no way of getting a lift or a bus back to your front door. Start gently, perhaps aiming to do no more than 2 miles (3.2 km) (which should take you between 40 minutes and an hour) on your first outing. You can then gradually increase your mileage as your fitness levels improve and your legs and feet get used to it.

Avoid sore feet...

... next to thirst, aching or blistered feet is the most demoralising experience for a walker. Remember though that blisters or other irritations of the feet are caused not by excessive walking but inappropriate footwear. If you're still at the beginning of your walking 'career' you don't need a pair of heavy walking boots, but at the other extreme, slippers, slip-ons and flipflops aren't appropriate either, nor is any fashion footwear. A pair of comfortable, stout outdoor shoes or trainers with robust chunky soles, protected by a pair of thick socks or two layers of thin socks, will be fine. Experiment a bit in the early days, deciding what feels comfiest. Just make sure that if you get attached to a particular pair of socks you put them in the wash once in a while!

In summary, then, in your early walks for pleasure:

- *Choose a fine day*
- *Clothe yourself sensibly*
- *Make sure your feet are comfortable*
- *Don't be over-ambitious*
- *Stick to roads, paths and tracks you know – or learn to map read!*
- *Take a bottle of water and some food*

… Now enjoy!

Now you've learnt what it is to be walking for pleasure, you can start to appreciate what's going on around you and what your immediate surroundings have to offer.

'When we walk, we are aware of the details around us – birds, trees, shops, houses, other people. We make connections.'
CARL HONORÉ, *IN PRAISE OF SLOW*

Play I-spy...

As we mentioned above, one of the great joys of walking is the ability to take things in at a much more leisurely pace than is possible when in the car, bus or train. With walking for pleasure comes the ability to notice so much more, including many features and phenomena you may either have taken for granted and/or never paid any real attention to before.

Look out for some of these on a short walk from home. How many did you know about before? (Note – some may only make seasonal appearances!)

An old house or cottage (look out for dates sometimes inscribed on the walls), especially one timbered or thatched ☐

An historic public building e.g. church or village school ☐

An unusual or distinctive building e.g. windmill ☐

Remains of a prehistoric construction e.g. earthwork or fort ☐

A ruin e.g. of a castle or abbey ☐

A wild flower or cluster of wild flowers e.g. buttercup, cowslip, primrose ☐

A wild rabbit, squirrel, fox or other non-domesticated animal ☐

Any tree or plant containing wild fruit e.g. apples, blackberries ☐

A butterfly with wings of more than one colour ☐

A bird with distinctive or colourful plumage ☐

The course of a former railway or canal ☐

An area of water or watercourse, particularly one supporting a variety of fish or other water creatures ☐

Walking is truly an all-the-year-round activity. There's the satisfaction and interest in watching the seasons change, the bare deciduous trees giving way to the lush new green leaves of spring, the abundance of March daffodils, the appearance of apple and cherry blossom and scent of wild garlic in April, the creamy white of hawthorn in May, the profusion of butterflies and insects on a languid summer's afternoon, the abundance of apples in orchards in late August, the golden and reddish hues of autumn, the flurry of autumn leaves cascading from the trees on a windy afternoon in woodland, a sharp frost coating the sun-drenched downland on a December morning, and the snow-capped hillsides of a winter's afternoon.

> *'And since to look at things in bloom,*
> *Fifty springs are little room,*
> *About the woodlands I will go*
> *To see the cherry hung with snow'*
>
> A. E. HOUSMAN

Q. What's the best area in Britain to enjoy wildlife with easy walking?

A. North Norfolk coast – there's a designated North Norfolk coast path between Hunstanton and Cromer, very easy walking all the way, and in the course of it you might see some, or all, of these birds, animals and insects:

Knot • curlew • dunlin • brent goose • Egyptian goose • starling • finch • skylark • redstart • flycatcher • bearded tit • marsh harrier • godwit • avocet • sandwich tern • little tern • common tern • ringed plover • grey plover • wryneck • wintering twite • snow bunting • shorelark • woodlark • brambling • fieldfare • red-throated diver • teal • wigeon • sanderling • snipe • oystercatcher • dragonfly • common seal • natterjack toad – how many of these did you spot on your Norfolk coast walk?

Create themed walks

You can broaden your appreciation of exploring in your local area by concocting themed walks of your own:

Try these themed walks:

- *Exploring all public footpaths within a 2-mile (3.2 km) radius of your home*
- *Following all rivers/watercourses within a 2-mile (3.2 km) radius of your home*
- *A walk linking all the pubs or cafes (or both!) in your home town*
- *A walk linking all the places of worship, past or present, in your home town*
- *A walk linking your local railway station with the next station*

For many the best kind of themed walking is wildlife and plantlife walking, wherever you are. Even in the throbbing metropolis that is London you can watch the wildlife and plantlife unfold through your walks during the year.

> *'I have desired to go where springs not fail,*
> *To fields where flies no sharp and sided hail,*
> *And a few lilies blow'*
> GERARD MANLEY HOPKINS

A London wildlife year

- A winter's day walk by the Lea Valley Reservoirs with sights of wintering birds such as gadwall, pochard, shoveler, goosander, smew and phalarope

- A spring walk through the daffodils of Lesnes Abbey Woods in Greenwich
- A bluebell walk through Kings Wood in Croydon
- Admiring the April/May flowering of catkins in the hornbeam woods of Epping, Hainault and Ruislip

- A summer afternoon's wander by the Thames watching for mute swan and mallard
- A balmy summer evening's stroll in Belgravia watching for the blackcap, goldfinch or spotted flycatcher, or a promenade in Highgate Cemetery watching for speckled wood butterfly, tawny owl, urban fox, hedgehog, badger or pipistrelle bat

- An autumn walk in one of the royal parks as the leaves change from green to red and gold, watching for heron and cormorant, great crested grebe or Canada goose on the park lakes, or goldcrest, nuthatch, kestrel, woodpigeon, pied wagtail, chaffinch, robin or woodpecker in the trees

Then back to Lea Valley and the cycle resumes...

'I never saw daffodils so beautiful – they grew among the mossy stones about and about them – some rested their heads upon these stones as on a pillow for weariness, and the rest tossed and reeled and danced and seemed as if they verily laughed with the wind that blew upon them over the lake.'

DOROTHY WORDSWORTH

Some tips and hints for walkers seeking flora and fauna

Do invest in some binoculars – inexpensive, easy to use and may enable you to identify wildlife you might otherwise have missed

Do make an early start – dawn is a marvellous time to observe wildlife

Don't take the plant to the book – take the book to the plant – there's no need to pick a plant to name it

Don't disturb animals or endanger rare plants

Do beware of scaring birds when they're nesting – species which appear to be tame may simply be reluctant to leave their eggs

Do watch you don't trample delicate plants when looking for other species

Do avoid disturbing species in the breeding season

Do remember that a quiet careful observer will see more wildlife than a noisy clumsy one

'What do we see at once but a little robin! There is no need to burst into tears fotherington-tomas swete tho he be.'

GEOFFREY WILLANS AND RONALD SEARLE, *DOWN WITH SKOOL*

Whatever walking you do, remember the Countryside Code.

The Countryside Code - Headline Messages

Code for the public
Respect Other People
1. Consider the local community and other people enjoying the outdoors
2. Leave gates and property as you find them and follow paths unless wider access is available

Protect The Natural Environment
1. Leave no trace of your visit and take your litter home
2. Keep dogs under effective control

Enjoy The Outdoors
1. Plan ahead and be prepared
2. Follow advice and local signs

Code for land managers
1. Know your rights, responsibilities and liabilities
2. Make it easier for visitors to act responsibly
3. Identify possible threats to visitors' safety
   Fuller explanations of these headline messages are available on the Countryside Code website.

Going further afield

Congratulations. You've completed your first few local walks. You may be happy with what you're doing, and not want to do any more than enjoy and appreciate your locality and the riches of history, wildlife and scenery it has to offer, perhaps on Sunday afternoon strolls. Many are happy never to do any more and still find joy in their walking.

On the other hand you may be hungry for more. But while you want some more purposeful walking, with more cultural and scenic rewards, you may not feel ready yet for more rugged or remote countryside, nor feel you have the ability to read maps or take compass bearings. The great news is that there are many fantastic and very rewarding walks available to those who may not have the confidence, experience and desire to trek into the moors and the mountains and who would prefer to stick to firm surfaces. We'll look at three examples of these now.

City walks

These really are 'win-win'. You'll be walking along pavements or pedestrian walkways, whether on streets or through parks and gardens, so you won't get muddy; roads and streets will all be signed so with the aid of a street plan you won't get lost; if it starts to rain there will be plenty of opportunities for shelter, and there'll be cafes and pubs to welcome you when you need a cuppa or a bite to eat. The chances are there'll be lots to see within a very short space, and if you do feel you've had enough and you're some way from the finish, you'll almost certainly find there's a bus that can get you back there.

In Britain we are blessed with many fine cities which contain a huge number of really notable features, easily covered during the course of a day's walk – overseas, even more so. The best bet is to head for the city's tourist information office. It's likely they will be able to provide, quite possibly free of charge, a map of the city centre with places of interest marked on it. Even a city that's not on the average tourist's bucket list will be likely to boast an interesting church, museum or park that's teeming with wildlife. Look out also for guided walks. The disadvantage of these is that you'll be travelling at the pace dictated by your guide, but since your guide will by definition be an expert on the ground s/he is covering, you will get to find out a great deal more about the places of interest that you pass. There are some terrific guided 'theme' walks you can do; for instance, many cities offer ghost walks at night, and guided walks are often laid on during city arts festivals.

Below we offer three city walks, all in England, to get you started – but there's no magic in the choice of cities or routes and you may feel tempted to detour and devise your own variations on the theme.

Three city walks to try

LONDON *(approximately 3 miles/4.8 km)*

*Starting from the **London Eye**, situated by the **Jubilee Gardens**, follow the South Bank of the **river Thames** downstream – at weekends and in summer this is a really vibrant area with its many stalls and attractions.*

*Pass Hungerford Bridge and the South Bank concert halls including the **Royal Festival Hall**, then pass Waterloo Bridge and the **National Theatre**.*

*Next comes the exuberant **Gabriel's Wharf** plaza, the **Oxo Tower** which houses modern shops, eateries and offices, and the ornate **Blackfriars Bridge**.*

*Go on to the **Tate Modern Art Gallery** and cross the Thames by the **Millennium Bridge**. Before crossing the bridge it's certainly worth detouring a very short way on downstream to view the thatched timber-framed reconstruction of the **Globe Theatre**, originally built by Shakespeare's company, the Lord Chamberlain's Men. Crossing the bridge will take you straight up to **St Paul's Cathedral**. Begun in 1675, the cathedral with its famous Whispering Gallery and its huge crypt with tombs of Nelson and Wellington, miraculously escaped destruction in the Blitz.*

Head westwards from the cathedral along Ludgate Hill into Fleet Street, passing **St Bride's Church** *with its so-called 'wedding cake' spire, the* **Royal Courts of Justice**, *and on along the Strand (possibly detouring to the right along Bedford Street to the bustling* **Covent Garden Market**, *for 300 years the chief market for fruit, vegetables and flowers in London; its name was originally Convent Garden from an old garden that belonged to the monks of Westminster Abbey). This takes you to* **Trafalgar Square** *and* **Nelson's Column**, *170 ft high with a 18 ft high statue of Nelson on top of it.*

Exit Trafalgar Square along Whitehall passing **Horse Guards Parade**, **Downing Street – the official residence of the Prime Minister since 1732**, *the early seventeenth century* **Banqueting House**, *(the first example in England of the new Classical style of architecture, introduced from Italy) and the* **Cenotaph**, *reaching Parliament Square, on the far side of which is* **Westminster Abbey**, *described as the most beautiful Gothic church in London.*

Turn eastwards from Parliament Square to pass the **Houses of Parliament** *and* **Big Ben**; *Big Ben isn't the bell tower but the actual bell, named after the First Commissioner of Works, Sir Benjamin Hall (the tower contains cells where MPs can be imprisoned for breach of parliamentary privilege) and cross* **Westminster Bridge**, *bearing left onto the riverbank past the huge old County Hall building to return to the London Eye.*

BATH (approximately 2 miles/3.2 km)

*From the station walk north up Manvers Street into Pierrepont Street, passing Parade Gardens and reaching the covered **Pulteney Bridge**, completed in 1773 and named after William Pulteney, reputedly the wealthiest man in Britain at that time.*

*Bear left here into Bridge Street, shortly bearing right into Northgate Street and then left into Broad Street, past the **Postal Museum**; at end bear left into George Street then right into Gay Street, bringing you to the eighteenth century **Circus,** off which is Bennett Street with its **Museum of East Asian Art** and **Fashion Museum**.*

*Head westwards along Brock Street to reach **Royal Crescent**, with its magnificent Regency architecture, the work of John Wood, the Younger, between 1767 and 1774.*

Retrace your steps via the Circus and Gay Street, going straight on this time, perhaps visiting the **Jane Austen Museum**, then continuing past Queen Square into Barton Street, bearing round left into Westgate Street and forward into Cheap Street.

Detour to the right to reach the square containing **Bath Abbey** (founded in 1499 by Bishop of Bath, Oliver King), the eighteenth-century **Pump Room**, and **Roman Baths**. These are among the best-preserved Roman remains anywhere in England, dating back almost 2,000 years, although the waters themselves, supposed to have healing qualities, were described in Dickens' Pickwick Papers as tasting like 'warm flat-irons'.

Pick up York Street on the south side of the Pump Room, following it eastwards past **Sally Lunn's House**, one of the oldest houses in Bath with Roman and medieval foundations, named after a Huguenot refugee (her name was Anglicised) who created a rich round bread named the Sally Lunn Bun. You arrive at Pierrepont Street, turning right to retrace your steps to the station.

YORK *(approximately 2 miles/3.2 km)*

*From the station turn left into Station Road, soon passing Leeman Road with the **National Railway Museum**, boasting over a hundred locomotives including one of the earliest, Puffing Billy, and the world's fastest steam locomotive, the Mallard.*

*Go round to the right, turning left at the crossroads and crossing **Lendal Bridge** continuing past **Lendal Tower** and along Museum Street, with Museum Gardens to the left housing the **Yorkshire Museum**.*

*Bear left round into St Leonard's Place and right into High Petergate, going forward into Minster Yard and Deangate, immediately adjoining **York Minster** which was built between 1220 and 1472 and has magnificent medieval stained glass windows.*

*Fork left to detour into the Minster precinct to visit **St William's College** in College Street, and, a bit further on, the seventeenth century **Treasurer's House** where ghosts of a Roman legion are still reputed to march through its cellars.*

Return to Deangate and follow it to Bedern Hall, turning right into Goodramgate, bearing left at the end and going straight on down the **Shambles**, *a street of timber-framed cottages where at one time there were twenty-six butchers' shops – or 'shambles' (derived from the word 'shamel', a shelf below a butcher's window where meat was sold).*

You arrive at Pavement and turn right to follow it. Go forward into Coppergate past the **Jorvik Viking Centre**, *a reconstruction of the sights, sounds and even smells of Viking York, built on the site where Viking remains were first discovered.*

Bear left into Clifford Street going forward into Tower Street, detouring off Clifford Street to visit the **York Dungeon** *and off Tower Street to visit the* **Regimental Museum** *and* **Clifford's Tower**, *the keep from the old castle, founded in 1068 and rebuilt in the thirteenth century. Just beyond is the* **York Castle Museum**, *which boasts a life-size replica of a Victorian street and the original cell where Dick Turpin was held.*

At the end of Tower Street turn right, crossing Skeldergate Bridge into Bishopgate Street, soon turning right to join the **city wall**. *The walls were built on Roman foundations and date from the twelfth century. Follow the wall clockwise parallel with Nunnery Lane and Queen Street to return to the station.*

Other cities easy and enjoyable to visit on foot

Oxford – Colleges, Christ Church Cathedral, Bodleian Library
Cambridge – Colleges, The Backs, Kings College Chapel
Cardiff – Castle, St David's Cathedral, Millennium Stadium
Durham – Cathedral, Castle, River Wear

And for the more ambitious among you… *Lonely Planet*'s Top Ten City Hikes

1. Tijuca Forest, Rio de Janeiro
2. Great Coastal Walk, Sydney
3. Thames Path, London
4. Hoerikwaggo Trail, Cape Town
5. Berlin Wall Trail, Berlin
6. Seawall, Vancouver
7. South Mountain Park, Phoenix
8. Coast to Coast Walk, Auckland
9. Arthur's Seat, Edinburgh
10. Hong Kong Trail, Hong Kong

'I wandered lonely as a cloud that floats on high o'er vales and hills.'
WILLIAM WORDSWORTH

Old railway walks

Early in the twentieth century, Britain enjoyed a very extensive network of country railways. However, many proved to be uneconomical to run and as a result, under the notorious British Rail chairman, Dr Beeching, vast numbers of rural railway lines were closed. Some were revived as preserved steam railways; some were left to their fate and were built on; but some have been turned into walkways for pedestrian and cycle use.

By definition they provide very easy walking: a firm surface, little or no climbing, and no navigational difficulties. And they have the advantage over city or town walks of being more peaceful, many passing through very beautiful countryside including farmland, woodland and rolling hill country. There is one catch – their starts and finishes aren't always easily accessible by public transport.

Try these (or parts of these!).
They're all superb examples of
this type of walking at its best.

Monsal Trail, Derbyshire – An 8.5-mile (13.6-km) walk from Blackwell Mill in Chee Dale, near Buxton, to Coombs Road at Bakewell, through beautiful Peak District countryside and with the added interest of four tunnels, each about 400 metres (433 yds) long, and two shorter tunnels.

Mawddach Trail, Gwynedd – A 9.5-mile (15.2-km) walk from Dolgellau to Barmouth in North Wales, following the southern edge of the Mawddach Estuary with great views towards Snowdonia.

East Grinstead to Groombridge, Sussex – A 10-mile (16-km) walk through beautiful East Sussex countryside with views to Ashdown Forest and the infant river Medway, passing Hartfield – famous for its Winnie the Pooh associations.

Rowrah Sculpture Trail, Cumbria – An 11.5-mile (18.4-km) walk from Whitehaven to Rowrah in Cumbria via Cleator Moor, noted for its sculptures reflecting the industrial heritage of the area, with views towards the Lakeland mountains.

Bristol and Bath Railway Path, Somerset – A 13-mile (20.8-km) walk between these two cities, close to the delightful river Avon and an important wildlife corridor. The restored Bitton station, sculptures at Warmley and a tunnel on the outskirts of Bristol are the highlights.

Brampton Valley Way, Northamptonshire – A 14-mile (22.4-km) walk from Boughton Crossing in Northampton to Little Bowden crossing, Market Harborough; a lovely rural walk through tranquil East Midlands countryside, the highlights being Brixworth Country Park and Pitsford Water.

Canalside walks

Canal usage declined with the coming of the railways, but in recent years many of Britain's canals have been restored for leisure use and there are some excellent walks available on canal towpaths, providing easy, level-walking through often very beautiful countryside. Navigation will certainly not be a problem as you'll have the canal beside you all the time.

Try these canal walks in full or in part:

- Regent's Canal, London – An 8.5-mile (13.6-km) walk from Little Venice to Limehouse in London, taking you through sections of the capital that you may well never have explored, including Camden Town, Islington, De Beauvoir Town, Haggerston, Victoria Park and Mile End – where North London meets East London.

- Leeds and Liverpool Canal – A 16-mile (25.6-km) walk along the Aire Valley towpath section between Leeds and Bingley, incorporating townscapes, lovely West Yorkshire countryside and some historic sites.

- Caledonian Canal – The section of Great Glen Way between Banavie, near Fort William on the west coast of Scotland, and Fort Augustus is some 28 miles (44.8 km) and follows sections of the Caledonian Canal interspersed with Lochs Lochy and Oich – very easy walking with superb mountain views including Ben Nevis.

- Montgomeryshire and Brecon Canal – this section of towpath of just over 30 miles begins at Brecon and ends at Cwmbran in south Wales; described as one of the most picturesque in the UK, it provides stunning views of mountains, most notably the Brecon Beacons, as well as lovely walking through river valleys and woodland. The towpath is in excellent condition with easy access to good pubs.

- Grantham Canal – This walk along the Grantham Canal towpath through the Vale of Belvoir in Nottinghamshire stretches for 33 miles (52.8 km) between Grantham and Nottingham and includes Cotgrave Country Park with a heron lake, woodland, wetland and grassland.

- Arguably the best British waterside walk of all is the Thames Path – the ultimate inland waterside walk in Britain. It follows the river Thames for most of its length, has excellent firm surfaces and navigation really couldn't be easier. But it's still a challenge for the walker, being 185-miles (296-km) long. Try it a bit at a time. See chapter 5 for more details.

Organised walks/walking clubs

If by now you want to be even more ambitious in your walking but still don't have the confidence to tackle more demanding routes either on your own, or with your companions, you could join a walking organisation.

The biggest walking organisation by far is the Ramblers. With your membership you will receive their quarterly magazine, with lots of described walks of varying degrees of difficulty plus plenty of articles about walking generally, advice on equipment etc., and you'll get details of the thousands of organised and guided walks that take place throughout the year. But there are many other ramblers' clubs as well, offering guided/group walks on which you're sure to increase your confidence as a walker, and possibly make some new friends along the way. You can access details of your local ones online or in your local public library.

If you prefer your 'more ambitious' walks in small doses but don't necessarily want to commit to an organisation, you could undertake a one-off programme of guided walks. A great way of facilitating this is through walking festivals: for example, in 2013 the North Devon and Exmoor Walking Festival offered walks as diverse as 'Explore the Tors', 'Flowerpot Men, Secret Coves and Old Mill' and 'Wild Food and Useful Plants'.

Did you know that...
Studies on the brains of older people have shown that keeping physically active can improve cognitive function, memory, attention and processing speed, and reduce the risk of cognitive decline and dementia.

And now you're ready for a walk on the wild side…

There ought to be a word for it...

Sense of guilt you feel deserting your partner and four children for walking holiday however well-earned, leading to over-solicitous phone call on first night away, presentation of over-generous gifts on return, and rash promise to take them all on a beach holiday somewhere intolerably hot and expensive

Disappointment on discovering bus needed to access proposed walk is limited to one every Wednesday morning excluding bank holidays

Feeling of utter bliss at removing your walking boots during mid-walk break

Amazement on discovering people you meet on a walk absolutely miles from nowhere and at least 300 miles from home live two streets away from you

Reluctance to bare arms or legs during hot day's walk for fear of exposing embarrassing tattoos you drunkenly had done in Southend two years ago

Heavy mid-walk meal, much enjoyed at the time, which then weighs so heavily on your stomach as you set off again that you wish you'd just stuck to the salad bar

Stage of challenging walk where your guide or Internet notes tell you 'This is where most walkers who are going to give up, do so'

Reaching what you believe is the top of the hill only to see another, much steeper hillside rising up behind it

Unspecified location in a distant galaxy, to which the single unused bootlace from a new pair of laces disappears, never to be traced when needed at a later date

Pleasing smell of newly unpacked expensive walking jacket, fresh from its cellophane wrapping

CHAPTER 4

WILDER WALKING

'On the top there are no signposts, no markers. Only the choice of channels between the chocolate-covered peat.'

JOHN HILLABY, *JOURNEY THROUGH BRITAIN*

You've enjoyed a potter in Bath, or a stroll by the Regent's Canal, or pretending to be a steam train puffing through the Peak District. And maybe it's the sight of all those hills in the Peak District or the hills rising up behind the Caledonian Canal that now makes you want to head for the hills and to tackle some of the wilder, more remote and mountainous countryside of Great Britain.

The good news – the rewards in terms of the scenery, the views and the greater variety of plant life and wildlife are massive. There is the enticing prospect of mountains soaring to over 4,000 feet (1,200 m), ridgetops and clifftops looking out across whole counties, sightings of golden eagle, osprey and puffin, and so much more.

The less good news – you need to be much better prepared. All the ground rules set out in the above chapters apply, but there are many more things you need to be aware of if your walk is to be a joy, and not a disaster.

Now it gets serious.

Wilder Walking Q & A

Q. What do we mean by wilder walking?

A. In this chapter we mean:

Hills and fells

Forests

Clifftops

Moorland

Mountains (Note – in this book we do not cover mountaineering but confine ourselves to ascents of mountains that can be managed with ordinary walking gear and without specialist mountain equipment such as ice axes, ropes, crampons etc.)

Wilder Walking Q & A

Q. What are the risks of wilder walking?

A. The walking is more strenuous – you need stamina

The terrain is tougher underfoot – you need decent footwear

The weather will be unpredictable – you need decent clothing

There will be fewer landmarks – you need to be able to map read and know where you are

There'll be fewer amenities – you need to bring food and drink

You may get into difficulties – you need to take precautions

You may have a lot to carry – you need a good rucksack

About stamina

It's a bad idea for your first walk, after years of not-so-blissful indolence, to be a ten-mile mountain hike. It's likely to end in tears. If you're a beginner you should follow all the steps and guidance given in chapter 3, doing lots of walking around your local area, building up your stamina levels until you're sure you can cope with more demanding walking. If your walking has been confined to level countryside, begin to factor in some gentle hillclimbing as well. You can practise in everyday life as well, using stairs instead of escalators or lifts. Then, as your confidence and stamina levels increase, you should go in for some more energetic hill climbing. There are plenty of easy and straightforward hill walks you can do, requiring no navigational skills, but choose a fine day for them!

It's important to cultivate good techniques for coping with steep ascents and descents in order to preserve stamina and fitness.

Top five tips for hill walking

1. Shorten your stride when ascending but move your legs at the same speed

2. Consider zigzagging on very steep hills – longer route but less arduous

3. Put the whole of the sole of the foot down on firm ground – avoid toe and heel holds

4. Don't be tempted to climb your first hill of the day too quickly

5. When descending steeply, allow the legs to bend slightly at the knee to avoid jarring the body

Diet is important as well when embarking on more or longer walks than you are used to. Your ability to cope with wilder walking will be affected if either you're not eating enough, or if you're badly overweight. You also need to ensure you eat properly before you set off on a wilder walk. The best sorts of food to include in your meals are those that fill you up but which release energy slowly into the body. Chat to your GP if you want more specific advice.

Always… have a good breakfast before setting off for the day.

Always… stop and eat something if you feel hungry. Your stamina levels will diminish frighteningly quickly if you've an empty stomach.

Always… ensure you have some rest times built into a day's walk to revive yourself.

> ***Top tip:*** *When you stop to rest, choose a spot out of the wind, remove your boots as well as your backpack, and after you've had something to eat and drink lie flat on your back and relax completely – this will help re-energise you both physically and mentally.*

Lastly, you mustn't try to do any more miles in a day than you know you're capable of.

Naismith's Formula may help

Allow one hour for every three miles (4.8 km) measured on a map plus an additional hour for every 2,000 ft (610 m) climbed. (Note: your walk may not include any single climbs of 2,000 ft but there may be cumulative ascent which far exceeds this).

Bear in mind that in poor conditions your pace may be significantly slower.

In practice it's better to aim to do a little less than you think you're capable of. That way you can build in time to enjoy the surroundings, and have the occasional rest.

Wilder Walking Q & A

Q.What's the best area in Britain to walk for spectacular wildlife finds?
A. The Cairngorms in North-East Scotland.

See in the Cairngorms:
Osprey on rivers and lochs (there's an observation hide at Loch Garten near Aviemore)
Golden eagle in the mountains
Ptarmigan in the mountains
Dotterel in the mountains
Peregrine in the mountains
Buzzard on moorland edges near woodland
Merlin on the moors
Red grouse on the moors
Ring ouzel on the moors
Snow bunting on the mountains
Capercaillie in the forests
Goldeneye around woodland lochs
Reindeer on the mountains
Red deer on the moors
Red squirrel in the forests
Wildcat in the forests
Fox in the forests
Badger in the forests
Otter in the forests

About decent footwear

While trainers or stout outdoor shoes will be fine for level tramping, and for short straightforward hill walks on firm surfaces, these are not sufficient when walking in wilder country.

The following are hazards you may meet underfoot:

- Clay soil – huge lumps can cling to the soles of your footwear
- Wet grass – can be very slippery on inclines
- Mud
- Loose stones/boulders – particularly on hillsides
- Rock covered with slime or lichen
- Peatbogs – a hazard on moorland
- Water – puddles, streams, even rivers which may need to be forded
- Snow and ice in winter

Just a handful of walks in which you encounter such hazards could tear your trainers to shreds.

You need proper walking shoes or boots which won't let in water, which can stand up to the punishment the above hazards may give, and which will be comfortable.

There is a formidable choice out there and it's difficult to know where to start.

Like everything in life, you get what you pay for. It's up to you whether you splash out on a hi-tech, ultra-durable pair for several hundred pounds from a specialist walking goods retailer but which last you forever, or whether you choose the cheapest pair on eBay, in a car boot sale or Millet's and find yourself having to replace them after six months. If you're serious about walking, but haven't got unlimited funds, you may want to go somewhere down the middle.

Top boot tips:

It's vital that you:

Get decent socks to go with them – loop stitch socks are recommended – and wearing two pairs means you get extra cushioning for the feet.

Break them in – meaning wear them around the house and for short easy walks before taking them out on a longer tougher walk. Breaking-in helps make them conform to the shape of the feet.

Try the boots on first (taking your walking socks with you), before committing yourself to buying. There should be enough room to poke a forefinger behind the heel and the toes should just touch the boot at the front. They must be 100 per cent comfortable. If they aren't, reject them. If they were ordered online and aren't comfortable, send them back. (In view of the hassle involved with this, boots are better purchased in shops rather than online.)

Clean them after each walk and apply dubbin (or equivalent) for protecting the fabric. Your boot retailer can advise of available products and how to apply them.

> **Did you know that...**
> When walking the coastline of Britain, John Merrill
> got through three pairs of boots – each of which had
> been broken in over 500 miles (800 km) first. He
> changed out of his first pair after wearing them to
> destruction – they'd done 3,800 miles (6,080 km)!

About decent clothing

The big difference when out wilder walking is that the weather is
likely to be much more unpredictable. The chances are you'll do a
lot of your wilder walking when on holiday and unless you're very
fortunate, some rain will be inevitable, particularly in the Lake District
or in western Scotland; generally the weather will be cooler in these
regions as well. What you put on must be able to stand up to the
worst weather. It could literally be a life-saver.

In colder, wetter weather, it's vitally important that you wear sufficient
clothes to keep warm, but that the clothes you do wear remain dry,
and free from moisture and sweat. Several thin layers on top is better
than one piece of clothing, whatever kind of walking you do. The most
important thing to get right, in terms of clothing, is the jacket.

Any jacket you wear for your wild walking needs to be *waterproof* and *breathable*. A breathable garment lets air in and lets sweat out. Ideally it should contain what's called a wicking fabric. Unlike, say, cotton which will absorb water and hang onto your sweat – making your clothing, and you, wet and unpleasantly clammy – a wicking fabric, such as polyester, picks up moisture and carries it away from your body, spreading it out, to evaporate easily on the outside of the fabric so you stay cool and dry. It's also suggested that your base layer should be a shirt of synthetic material which will wick moisture from the body and reduce chilling.

> ***Top tip:*** *Before embarking on serious walking, seek advice on boots and clothing from a specialist outdoor retailer. Shop around for best value for money but remember you get what you pay for.*

About map reading/knowing where you are

Unless you know the terrain very well, it is folly to set out on any unguided walk in countryside you don't know without a map. You cannot rely on signposting alone; it only takes one damaged or non-existent signpost at a path junction to render you completely lost. If conditions are poor, the consequences could be serious.

The choice of maps is bewildering but for the walker by far and away the best is the orange-covered Ordnance Survey Explorer series. They cover the whole of Great Britain at a scale of 1:25,000 (roughly two and a half inches to a mile or 4 cm to 1 km) and given the amount of detail on them they are astonishingly good value for money.

The Explorer maps show, among many other things:

- All footpaths, bridleways and byways to which the public have access, either unrestricted or permissive
- Field boundaries
- Contours showing relative height
- Access land
- Places of particular scenic or historic interest or importance
- Lines marking the National Grid (meaning that if you select any landmark on the map, you can determine its location as a 'grid reference') (Instructions on how to ascertain a grid reference are given on each map key)

It is not only a good idea but essential, having decided on a wild walk, to trace it on a map, in conjunction with the key provided with each map.

Tracing your route will make you aware of:

- Availability of rights of way/access land for the walk you want to do
- Hazards close to or on your chosen route
- Landmarks which will help you navigate
- Distance and, using Naismith's formula (see p. 80), how long it'll take you

When conditions are clear and the path is well defined, you can confidently navigate with a map alone. However you may be caught in mist or fog, particularly on higher ground, and lose all sense of direction. When this happens, you'll need a compass or the use of GPS to get you out of trouble.

The compass is the low-tech option, tried and tested over centuries, not reliant on batteries or signals. It is also harder to use! There are different kinds of compass, and to find out how to use yours, either refer to the instructions accompanying it or go online – or both.

GPS: (Global Positioning System), GPS is a network of over twenty earth-orbiting satellites that beam signals to earth. The system enables you to determine your position and desired direction of travel at the touch of a few buttons of a hand-held device. GPS is reliant on your obtaining a signal, their accuracy may be compromised by large areas of water or thick tree cover, and they'll be no help at all if your device isn't charged. But if it works as it should it's much easier than taking a compass bearing; it's very reliable and much less fiddly.

GPS can do one of two things for you – tell you where you are, by means of a grid reference on your map, or provide, with an arrow, the most direct route, and mileage, to where you want to go – again, by means of a grid reference on your map – and how far from it you are. It's a very easy system to operate – an outdoor store retailer can explain it to you in minutes – but it's essential you familiarise yourself with the grid referencing system first, using the instructions shown on the key of every Ordnance Survey Explorer map.

A walking hobby with a GPS device - geocaching

Geocaching has become a very popular pursuit, thanks to GPS. It involves seeking out and finding, using map references and the GPS device, a 'cache' usually consisting of a robust box buried in the ground, in a tree, in a summit cairn or other suitable place out of view, containing some goodies, e.g. food items/toys, and a means of logging your find. There's a strong geocaching etiquette - if you take something, you leave something behind. Some items may be passed from one cache to another, making its own journey round the country. It's a bit like a treasure hunt, combining fresh air and exercise with some detective work, and is an obsession for some; it's not unknown for geocachers to have clocked up several hundred caches. So, google 'geocaching' and join in the fun, adding another dimension to your walking enjoyment!

About food and drink

During the town and city walks you did, you'd have been spoilt for choice as far as refreshment opportunities went. However, there aren't too many branches of Costa in the wilds of the Peak District or the Brecon Beacons.

It is essential, whether you hope or expect to pass a cafe or pub en route, that when out wild walking you have not only plenty of bottled water with you but also food supplies. On cold days, a thermos with a hot drink is advisable as well.

Food for Thought

- *That cafe or pub you earmarked might be shut*
- *There may be no cafes or pubs on your route*
- *You may need to replenish your energy levels at a time when you're far away from any amenities*
- *Eating and drinking out is expensive – you can buy a thermos flask for little more than the price of a couple of takeaway coffees*

Ensure the food you take is rich in energy and fills you up. Hunger, like thirst, is demoralising and could disastrously diminish your stamina levels. The energy boost provided by sugary snacks such as chocolate bars or cakes will be temporary; anything that dramatically increases your blood sugar level will result in a rebound sugar low, which gives you an energy slump. Instead, opt for healthy snacks such as nuts and fruit, especially bananas which are rich in potassium and provide slow-releasing energy. Protein is also very good for walkers, giving you energy throughout the day.

A (slightly) naughty tip – If you can't resist sweet treats for a fix of energy, try Kendal Mint Cake. It's not cake at all, but very sweet minty confectionery and very refreshing, beloved of hill walkers. Just don't tell your dentist…

About precautions

Most wild walks are accomplished without difficulty or incident. But sometimes bad things happen.

The Four Last Things (that you want to happen on a wild walk)

- Injury
- Illness or exhaustion
- Getting lost
- Deterioration in weather or light

Prevention is of course, better than cure:

- Avoid risk of injury by being careful and sensible, being properly booted and clad, and being vigilant for obstacles and hazards. If you feel unwell at the start of the day, consider if it's sensible to go out.
- Avoid the risk of exhaustion by following the advice given in relation to stamina levels and taking supplies of food and drink with you for consumption when needed. Never set out to do more than you can comfortably manage in a day.
- Avoid getting lost by being proficient in map reading, compass and/or GPS.
- Don't go out, or be prepared to curtail your walk, if there is a risk of bad weather or you are short on daylight.

 Top tip from the doyen of Lakeland mountain walking Alfred Wainwright: simply, watch always where you are putting your feet. If you want to admire the view, stop and then admire it.

But even then, things can go wrong. So:

- Ensure you're equipped with a first-aid kit including a supply of bandages and plasters. A torch is also advisable if there is any risk of being caught out by the darkness.
- Have your mobile phone and make sure it's fully charged before you go out walking, leave your details with someone and in turn take their details, so you have a source of help if you do get stranded.

Top tip: *In the event of your mobile phone failing, the recognised distress signal is six blasts of a whistle repeated at one minute intervals.*

About rucksacks

Even if you're just going out for a day's wild walking, there'll be a fair bit to take with you. There'll be essentials such as cash/plastic, food, drink, first aid kit, phone and any other appropriate emergency equipment; your map, also compass or GPS device; and you may find you have spare clothing with you that you don't need on all the time, but you need to have with you just in case.

Clearly you can't carry these things about with you in a five pence M & S bag, and you will need a rucksack, big enough to accommodate what you need, but not so big that you're tempted to take a lot of stuff you don't need. The benefit of a rucksack is that it enables the weight of your load to be spread evenly and enables you to retain a good posture, ensuring that the weight on your shoulders is kept to a minimum.

Once again, you get what you pay for, but any rucksack must be capable of fitting comfortably on your back, with straps that adjust so as to reduce the weight on your shoulders, and be able to keep the contents dry.

Where to go?

So – you've equipped yourself, and you're raring to go. But where to go?

In Great Britain alone we are blessed with an amazingly wide variety of countryside, catering for the tastes of every walker. It's difficult to know where to start, but a great place to choose as the base for your wild walking in Britain is one or more of the National Parks. Here we offer a particular jewel for each crown.

The current National Parks of the United Kingdom

In England

Yorkshire Dales – James Herriot country, limestone cliffs, impressive fells interspersed with beautiful valleys such as Swaledale and Wensleydale (try the ascent of Whernside – described in full below)

Lake District – England's highest peaks and a host of other fells and mountains around the unforgettably beautiful lakes of Derwent Water, Ullswater, Wastwater and many more (try Haystacks from Buttermere, with astonishing views and the last resting place of Alfred Wainwright)

Peak District – the White Peak, lush rolling green hills and picturesque dales, the Dark Peak, forbidding yet magnificent peat moorland (try the Kinder Plateau and the Kinder Low viewpoint)

Exmoor – steep heather-clad hills and beautiful woodland, immortalised by R. D. Blackmore in the classic novel *Lorna Doone* (try Dunkery Beacon, the summit of Exmoor and Somerset)

Dartmoor – windswept, wild moorland, characterised by stony hilltops called tors (try High Willhays, the highest point in southern England – described in full below)

Northumberland - huge forests, the Cheviot hills rising to over 2,600 feet (792 m) and Hadrian's Wall (yes, try Hadrian's Wall, large sections of which have been miraculously and splendidly preserved)

North York Moors - heather moorland, sweeping views and some of the best cliff scenery on the East coast of Britain (try Roseberry Topping, the distinctive peak on the Cleveland Way)

Norfolk and Suffolk Broads - these lakes and wetlands of East Anglia are a magnet for wildlife and plant life (try a stroll round the wetland habitats of Hickling Broad National Nature Reserve near Potter Heigham)

South Downs - rolling chalk downland with sensational views to the Weald and the sea (try walking from Hassocks to Ditchling Beacon with its amazing Wealden views - described in full below)

New Forest - not only forest but fine coastal scenery with beautiful views to the Isle of Wight (try walking beside the River Beaulieu from Buckler's Hard with its maritime museum and timeless waterside setting to Beaulieu with its Cistercian Abbey)

In Scotland

The Cairngorms – numerous mountains over 4,000 feet (1,300 m) and two fine rivers, the Dee and the Spey (try a section of the Speyside Way especially round Glenlivet and its association with whisky)

Loch Lomond and the Trossachs – classic Scottish Highland scenery (try the lochside walk from Balmaha to Ardlui on the West Highland Way)

In Wales

Snowdonia – the highest mountain of England and Wales, numerous lakes, magnificent coastal scenery (try Snowdon, the highest point of Wales)

Pembrokeshire Coast – some of the most stunning cliff scenery in Britain (try the walk along the Pembrokeshire Coast Path between St David's Head and St David's)

Brecon Beacons – flat-topped mountains rising to nearly 3,000 feet (914 m), contrasted with the peace and beauty of the Monmouthshire & Brecon Canal (try the ascent of Pen-y-Fan, the summit of the Beacons)

Three bits of National Park trivia:

- The National Parks of Britain currently receive over 150 million day visits a year
- The most visited are Lake District and Peak District
- The least visited are Northumberland and Exmoor – why not give them a visit to see what everyone's missing out on?

Try these wild National Park walks

Below are three wild walks for you to try, all in National Parks, very contrasting in nature and representing different parts of the country, and all hugely enjoyable. They aren't technically difficult and can each be easily accomplished in a day, but they are strenuous, they demand respect, and you need to be fit and follow the instructions given above. They're all circular walks starting from places served by public transport.

A wild walk on the South Downs to Ditchling Beacon, the highest point in East Sussex – 6 miles (9.6 km). Start – Hassocks station, West Sussex

From **Hassocks station** walk briefly down the station approach road then opposite the pub turn right down a flight of steps to meet the main street (B2116). At the bottom, cross the road, turn right and walk towards the **railway bridge**; as you reach the bridge you meet two signed paths in close succession going off to the left. Ignore the first but take the second which for just over a mile runs parallel with and just to the left of the railway, ending by the junction of the B2112, coming in from the left, with the A273. Cross straight over the B2112 and follow a signed path over a **sports field**, aiming for the right-hand side of the clubhouse, then beyond the clubhouse join the approach road taking you very shortly to **Clayton village street**. You need to cross straight over onto a signed bridleway heading southwards, but it's worth detouring to the right to see two features of **Clayton**. One is the extraordinary brick baronial entrance to **Clayton tunnel** on the London to Brighton line, and the other is the **village church**, which boasts a pre-1066 chancel arch and superb medieval wall paintings. Keith Spence in his Companion Guide To Kent And Sussex bemoans the fact that they have 'had to contend with being spattered by bat droppings!'

Now proceed along the **bridleway** south of the village street. Ignore a signed (yellow arrow) footpath going off to the left, and continue along the obvious signed (**blue arrow**) bridleway which now gains height quickly, heading steeply south-eastwards. Now look out for the two **windmills**, Jack and Jill, to your right, and aim for the clear path skirting the north-east side of the mills. Of the two,

Jill, the right-hand one as you look at them, is undoubtedly the more attractive and photogenic with its sails and bright white colour; the darker Jack, to the left, is something of a poor relation, lacking any sails! Jack is the tower of a smock mill whereas Jill is a post mill, built in 1821 and actually hauled here from Brighton in 1850 – by oxen.

*Having paused to enjoy the mills, keep along the path, arriving at a T-junction where you turn left onto a clear track heading south-eastwards. Very shortly the **South Downs Way** comes in from the right, and you now follow the South Downs Way all the way to **Ditchling Beacon**. Initially, you continue to climb, keeping the fence to your left, then you veer gently left, from south-eastwards to just north of east, now on top of the scarp. The East Sussex/West Sussex border spur of the **Sussex Border Path** comes in, also from the right (although it isn't signed) and then shortly goes off to the left. Now enjoying magnificent views, continue along the top of the scarp, passing just to the right of clumps of bushes and one of the characteristic **dewponds** of the South Downs Way (SDW); you shortly pass to the left of another dewpond, then begin a very clear and quite stiff climb, signalling your approach to the climax of the walk. As you climb, you keep a fence to your right. The fence bends sharply to the right and immediately beyond this bend you'll see the **trig point** above you to the right. Now simply make your way to it. The trig point does provide a tremendous panorama, stretching across the Downs for miles in both directions, the Weald to the north, and the sea to the south. In 1588 one of a chain of big fires was lit here to warn of the Spanish Armada's approach.*

*From the trig point, make your way back to the SDW and just continue a little further east to enjoy a superb view to **Blackcap**, the next big summit on the **South Downs**.*

*Now you head back towards **Hassocks** along the SDW, initially downhill then along the top of the escarpment, rising very steadily* to the wooden signpost known as **Keymer Post**, roughly a mile from Ditchling Beacon. Turn right here onto the signed bridleway which heads steeply downhill, then in roughly half a mile veers right. At this point, fork left onto a signed path which descends through the trees to reach **Underhill Lane**, going straight over to follow a grassy path which veers to the right, keeping an attractive lake to the right. Follow the signed path through the meadow, then as the lake veers away to the right and you get within sight of the eastern end of the meadow, veer round to the left and walk up to a gate at the top end, beyond which you go forward to arrive at **Lodge Lane**. Turn left to follow it down to the B2112 **New Road**, crossing straight over and following it, arriving at the B2116 in the centre of **Keymer**, passing a particularly fine thatched and timbered cottage just before the junction. Keymer boasts some other fine buildings including (by detouring very briefly right) the partially timber-framed **Greyhound Inn** and the part-Norman church of **St Cosmas and St Damian**. Your route is left at the junction, past **Keymer Manor House**, a four-bay aisled fouteenth century medieval house. Now follow the road to Hassocks with its good range of shops and cafes, bearing right along the station approach road to arrive at the station.

A wild walk in North Yorkshire – the ascent of Whernside, the highest point in North Yorkshire and one of the so-called Three Peaks – 7 miles (11.2 km). Start – Ribblehead Station, North Yorkshire

*Walk down the station approach slip road. Turn right onto the B6255 **Hawes-Ingleton road** and pass the pub, then very shortly bear left along a signed bridleway; proceed on the wide bridleway north-westwards, parallel with the railway, then veer left under the **Ribblehead viaduct**. This magnificent construction was completed between 1870 and 1875. Go forward north-westwards along the bridleway, veering westwards to **Gunnerfleet Farm** and passing the farm buildings to reach a T-junction with a track. Turn left onto it, then very shortly bear right along a signed footpath, keeping a wall to the right; go over a ladder stile and into the next field, going half-left across this field aiming for a little gate in the wall. Proceed through the gate into the adjacent field and follow the wall, heading north-westwards uphill. Use stone slabs to cross a wall and go forward across the next field, the path indicated by the darker grass, bringing you to the buildings of **Ivescar**. Ignore a signed bridleway going hard left but go forward into the farm area itself, and arrive at a clear bridle track pointing north-east/south-west. Turn left onto it, heading south-westwards, ignoring an early fork to the right. The track is well defined initially; it reaches a gate and veers gently right, and is then rather less well defined as it veers gently left and goes forward to another gate. Beyond it, continue in pretty much the same direction to reach the buildings of **Broadrake** which are to your right and, sticking to the same direction, continue beyond Broadrake across a field to* reach a signed path junction. Turn right here along the path signed '**Whernside** a mile and three quarters'.

The taxiing is now over, and you begin the assault on **Whernside** on what is a very clear path indeed, narrow but easily discernible all the way up. It is rocky and exceedingly steep in places, but the views just get better all the time. Eventually, it veers to the right, the gradient lessens, and you find yourself on the ridge. It's then a very exciting ridgetop walk to the summit triangulation point, and although the triangulation point itself is just behind a wall, you certainly won't miss it however bad the weather is. The views are magnificent; **Pen-y-Ghent** and **Ingleborough** are the most distinctive and conspicuous features, but the **Ribblehead viaduct** is also clearly visible, while to the north-west the verdant **Dentdale** provides a fine contrast to the stark steep hillsides.

Continue on beyond the summit along the ridge, sticking to the obvious main path, then within sight of the pools known as **Whernside Tarns**, you veer north-eastwards and drop down steeply round the side of **Great Knoutberry Hill**. Veering south-eastwards, you keep on an obvious path which continues to descend and arrives at a T-junction of paths. Turn right to follow the path south-eastwards, looking out for a lovely waterfall just to your right. Shortly you reach the railway and cross over it, but immediately to your right is a remarkable feature, a stone aqueduct carrying the stream that flows from the waterfall. Now keeping the railway to your right, and enjoying superb views to **Ingleborough** ahead, continue downhill past the **Blea Moor** signal box, arriving at a junction with the bridleway you were on at the start, close to the viaduct. You've come full circle and it now simply remains for you to turn left onto the bridleway and walk back to Ribblehead station.

***A wild walk on Dartmoor to High Willhays, the summit
of Dartmoor and the highest ground in southern
England – 9 miles (14.4 km) (NB – you can shorten the
walk to 6 miles (9.6 km) by taking a car or taxi to point
(1) below) Start: White Hart, Okehampton, Devon***

*From the **White Hart Hotel** in the centre of Okehampton, walk away from
the main street up **George Street** adjacent to the hotel. The road bends
slightly left; you see a church on the left, and more or less opposite the
church you turn right up **Station Road**, and follow it uphill. There's a left
turn signed to the old Okehampton Station but don't follow this; rather,
carry straight on uphill, passing over the old railway and also the A30.
There's a very sharp right-hand bend and then it's a straightforward road
walk until you reach a small parking area on the right-hand side and the
public road effectively ends (1). A right turn here leads to **Okehampton
Camp**, while roads leading away to the left are accessible to vehicles on a
permissive basis only. Bear left and then immediately right along a tarmac
track, keeping **Moor Brook** immediately to your left and a wall to your
right. Keeping the modest **Row Tor** to your left, remain on the tarmac track
up to a junction, with the tarmac track veering sharply left and a rougher
track continuing ahead. Go straight over onto this rougher track, keeping
West Mill Tor, appreciably higher than Row Tor, to your left. Follow this
rougher track onto **Black Down**, as far as a junction of paths level with a
col between **West Mill Tor** and its neighbour **Yes Tor** to the right, higher
still than West Mill Tor. Turn left at this junction.*

*You now follow what is quite a well-defined path fairly gently
uphill across the moor. The gradient then gets stiffer and the ground*

underfoot squelchier, as you make your way up to the col between West Mill Tor and Yes Tor. When the ground levels out, look carefully for a crossroads of paths more or less level with the stones on **West Mill Tor** which are to your left. Turn right here and now follow a path towards **Yes Tor**; it's fairly faint in places, but the path is more clearly defined up the hillside, so simply use that as a line. Initially the going is quite easy and remains so as far as **Red-a-ven Brook** which you have to ford, taking care as the stones around the brook may be quite slippery. Beyond the brook is the hardest work of the walk, as you climb very steeply to the summit of **Yes Tor** (grid reference for GPS - SX 580901), but you'll be amply rewarded. The summit is marked not only by stones but a triangulation point, and the views are astonishing, especially over **Dartmoor** but also northwards over mid-Devon towards Exmoor. It's only when you reach the summit of Yes Tor that the summit of **High Willhays** (grid reference for GPS - SX 580892) becomes apparent and the path to it, heading just west of south, is very obvious. Thankfully the col separating the two peaks is extremely shallow so the going is very easy. You descend gently and at the bottom of the descent, look out for a clear track going away to the left; don't follow it yet, but mark it, as you'll need it for the return journey! The track, meantime, climbs up, again quite gently, to arrive on the **High Willhays plateau**. There is a fair array of stones and boulders on the plateau but the proper summit is very clear, marked by a large cairn.

Now you need to make your way off the top, and return to the junction with the clear track referred to in the paragraph above (GPS - SX 580899); in clear weather this will be very easy, but in mist it could be a great deal harder. Having reached the track at the col, turn right to follow it. It drops quite gently, keeping **Yes Tor** to your left, and reaches the same beck that you forded earlier; again you need to ford it, and then continue on the clear stony track. Even if the mist prevented you enjoying the views on the summits, you should be luckier now, the views are quite magnificent not only to other tors of Dartmoor and their rock-strewn tops, but the rolling green fields of mid-Devon stretching on forever. The journey may be enlivened even further by the sight of **Dartmoor ponies**. The track continues very obviously, keeping **West Mill Tor** to the left and **Row Tor** to the right; don't be tempted onto a track snaking to the right on the nearside of Row Tor. The track becomes tarmac, and it's now simply a matter of following it back to point (1) above and retracing your steps to **Okehampton**, be it by car or on foot.

'I come from haunts of coot and hern
I make a sudden sally;
And sparkle out among the fern
To bicker down a valley.'

ALFRED, LORD TENNYSON

Munro or Marilyn?

If you're looking for a wild walking challenge in the British Isles you could become a peak bagger, building up 'collections' of hill or mountain tops you've managed to scale.

Munros

Named after the mountaineer Hugh Munro, these are the 282 mountains in Scotland that exceed 3,000 feet (914.4 m) above sea level. Munro-bagging is very popular among keen walkers and over 4,000 people have bagged them all. Some are tougher than others and some are very tough indeed, not to be attempted save by experienced, fit and properly equipped hill walkers, especially in bad weather or in winter.

Marilyns

A Marilyn is a hilltop with an overall drop of at least 150 metres (492 ft) on all sides. Therefore even a very lofty peak (peak 1) will not be a Marilyn if there is a peak immediately adjacent (peak 2) which is higher – unless it is necessary to drop more than 150 metres from the top of peak 1 to arrive at the base of peak 2. It follows, then, that in low-lying areas there will be some Marilyns of quite modest elevation, easily within the capability of even relatively inexperienced hillwalkers. There are no fewer than 2,009 of them in the British Isles.

Wainwrights

These are the 214 Lake District fells described in the pictorial guides of Alfred Wainwright (whom we'll meet again in chapter 6). You may bag only a few at a time but that gives you an excuse to keep coming back to the Lake District, providing the most stunning mountain and lake scenery in England.

County Highs

The highest points of every county or administrative region in Great Britain. Pre-1974, British counties were straightforward to find on a map but the establishment of unitary authorities has massively complicated things. However, complete lists are available in book form and on the Internet, and bagging them all provides a worthy objective for the hillwalker, as well as walks of remarkable variety – from the modest ascent of Beacon Hill in Norfolk to the grandeur of Mickle Fell in County Durham or Scafell Pike in Cumbria. In between there are such gems as Worcestershire Beacon in the Malvern Hills, Cleeve Hill in the Cotswolds and even Hampstead Heath, the highest point in Inner London with stunning views across the capital.

Did you know that...
In 2006 Jonny Muir in three months visited the ninety-one historic county tops of the British Isles in a 5,000 mile (8,000 km) walk.
   And in 2010 Alan Hinkes – the first Briton to climb the fourteen highest peaks on the planet – scaled the highest points of the thirty-nine traditional counties of England in eight days in a continuous walk starting at the Cheviot and ending on Helvellyn.

Just because it's not in a National Park or isn't a peak doesn't mean it's not worth exploring. Armed with your map, your equipment and the advice above, you can build up your own portfolio of wild walks and learn to love the immense variety of the scenery of Great Britain, and, with appropriate mapping and guidebooks, do the same overseas – through the joy of walking.

Did you know that...
There was only one hill Alfred Wainwright decided was not worth climbing. (Black Hill, West Yorkshire, on the Pennine Way)

There ought to be a word for it...

Keen walker's Christmas slide show, a cherished but paradoxically dreaded tradition amongst his nearest and dearest, consisting of many years' worth of inferior images projected using outdated or wholly unreliable technology

Post-Christmas-lunch walk organised by a keen walker for his family and house guests, inevitably far longer than any of them have walked in a single stretch this year

Involuntary reliving by insomniac of his long and tiring previous day's walk, so that by the time morning comes he's re-walked it twenty-eight times

Disappointment mingled with huge anti-climax that you feel on successfully reaching end of very long and challenging walk and finding everyone in your destination town or village going about their business without any recognition of you or what you've achieved

Chagrin on finding you're half a stone heavier after long walk than you were before it, on account of mixed grill, death by chocolate and two bottles of wine with which you celebrated its completion

State of total denial into which you move on reaching fog-enveloped hilltop after a four-hour climb, in which you refuse to believe that the fog is not only still there but if anything is even thicker than when you started

Urge, having reached a particularly great viewpoint or other famous landmark on your walk, to use your mobile to smugly ring a work colleague who you know is hard at work and tell them what a great time you're having

Sense of infuriation when scheduled televised Wainwright walk is postponed owing to over-running of friendly inter-national football match

Unavoidable sense of smugness you feel when enjoying walking holiday in utterly remote, unspoilt countryside and seeing newspaper picture of heatwave crowds packed on Brighton beach with no more than one square metre of space per person

Expression of disappointment that the first person to sign your marathon walk sponsor form pledges 50 pence on completion of the whole expedition

CHAPTER 5

LONG-DISTANCE WALKING

'I staggered on as if in a dream… Why had my boots become lead weights and my legs turned to jelly?'

ALAN PLOWRIGHT, *PLOWRIGHT FOLLOWS WAINWRIGHT*

'There must be something about long-distance walking that compels some people to keep trekking when they'd be better advised to quit.'

PADDY DILLON, *THE NATIONAL TRAILS*

So far we've only really considered day-length walks. Now we turn to the many opportunities available both in Britain and abroad for you to put together several days' walking and accomplish one of the many long-distance routes that have been devised and mapped by walkers past and present.

Before looking at the long-distance routes available, we need to consider the practicalities of walking on several consecutive days. Undertaking and completing the challenge of a long-distance walk is a very satisfying experience for a walker but it is not a challenge to be undertaken lightly.

To successfully complete a long-distance walk requires you to combine all the walking skills detailed in chapters 3 and 4 together with three others:

- A high level of physical fitness
- Excellent organisation
- The right equipment

A high level of physical fitness

We've already looked at the importance of building up your stamina levels but there's a difference between a single day's or afternoon's strenuous walk which you can recover from over time, and having to get walking again the next morning. You don't need to be super-fit to complete a long-distance route, but it stands to reason that if your route of choice is 180 miles (288 km) and you can only manage 5 miles (8 km) a day it's going to take you an awfully long time to complete it. Unless you're happy to take that long over a single path, you need to improve your daily quota, doing this by regular, frequent walking, ensuring your footwear is not only appropriate but comfortable, endeavouring as far as possible to replicate the terrain you're likely to meet on your route of choice (including carrying the equivalent weight and volume of equipment you'll need), and following the advice on sensible eating – to ensure not only that your body is up to it but you eat sensibly while out on the walks themselves. Your training regime should include a number of consecutive days' walking so you get used to the discipline of walking day after day after day.

Excellent organisation

Planning a long-distance walk is hugely enjoyable but it must be done sensibly.

Before you even start, get hold of maps and a guidebook covering your route of choice. Aurum and Cicerone publish guides, including maps, for all the major long-distance routes in Britain. If they've done one for your route of choice, buy or borrow it. Another option is to download information from the Internet but this may well not be as convenient for you to use when planning several days' walking at once.

Now you need to consider carefully:

- How many consecutive days' walking are available to you?
- How many miles you think you can manage on each of them?

You'll have a good idea from your training regime how many miles you can comfortably walk in a day, given the terrain you're up against. It's folly to overestimate your daily mileage simply in order to try to complete a long-distance route in a single expedition. You may end up overdoing it and having to give up halfway through. Better to aim to do a manageable amount in the time available then look forward to returning to it in a few months. Remember – it's not going to go away!

Of course there's nothing to stop you doing the whole of a long-distance route in separate day excursions, but you may feel the continuity will suffer and if you live a long way from the route you may spend more in petrol and fares than on accommodation.

If you decide to do several consecutive days' walking on a long-distance route, there will inevitably be some days that require you to do more mileage than others because of the availability of accommodation or public transport at particular points.

There are some long-distance routes where 'staging posts' are very many miles apart with no public transport, amenities or accommodation in between, and where you would have to walk many miles to obtain them. Such as:

- On Glyndwr's Way – 28 miles (45 km) between Llanidloes and Machynlleth
- On the Southern Upland Way – 27 miles (43 km) between St John's Town of Dalry and Sanquhar
- On the Pennine Way – 27 miles (43 km) between Byrness and Kirk Yetholm

Accommodation is of course a matter of personal taste. Camping costs next to nothing and allows you to be wholly independent, but after a long day's walking you may not relish the idea of pitching a tent, particularly in bad weather. At the other extreme, a luxury hotel provides the perfect chance to unwind but will do your budget no favours. Many walkers opt for something in-between, either youth hostelling or a B & B. Youth hostels aren't the formidably Spartan establishments they once were with their dour wardens, compulsory morning duties, lack of creature comforts and strict rules, and are excellent value for money. Many lasting walking friendships have sprung from youth hostel life. (For avoidance of doubt, don't be put off by the word 'youth' as anyone's eligible to stay in British 'youth' hostels!) B & Bs will offer friendly hospitality, a comfortable room and a terrific breakfast to set you up for your day's walk. Many establishments, of whatever type of accommodation, accept online bookings. It's advisable to book ahead to avoid spending time at the end of a long day's walk looking for a place to stay.

Distance learning – four top tips

Top tip 1: When booking your B & B, check how far it is from the route of your path – you don't want to add a lot of dead mileage to your daily quota!

Top tip 2: Make sure you have with you a piece of paper with the addresses and phone numbers of your accommodations, and if you're relying on lifts or public transport, relevant contact numbers and times. And keep the piece of paper in a safe place!

Top tip 3: Always think and plan ahead; think about when you might need supplies and where you're going to get them. If it's clear from your map or guide that there's going to be nowhere to buy food or drink during your day's walk, stock up beforehand.

Top tip 4: Investigate whether, if you're undertaking one of the more popular long-distance walks, a bag-carrying service is available – you will certainly make faster progress if you're not having to carry all your equipment.

The right equipment

In chapter 4 we considered what you'll need to take with you on a day's wild walking, and all that – and more – applies when you're walking for several days at a time and are away from home. You'll need a much bigger rucksack, with a belt round your middle so you're not carrying the weight on your shoulders. Then you'll need your checklist to help you load it up.

Your long-distance walk equipment checklist

Maps/guidebook(s) plus any
necessary navigation device with
charger/batteries as appropriate
Cash/plastic/cheque book
Mobile phone with charger
Camera
Contact/accommodation details
Food supplies
First-aid kit plus other
emergency kit e.g. whistle, torch
Changes of clothing/footwear
Toiletries
Binoculars
Sunglasses
Sunblock/sun hat
Colder weather: gloves/scarf/woolly hat
Diary/journal to record your
experiences – and pen/pencil
And – if you've decided to camp –
all your camping equipment.

A word to the wise: If having loaded all these into your rucksack you can't lift it up off the floor, don't panic. Take out everything you feel you can manage without. If after that you still can't lift it up off the floor – then you can panic…

How to lighten that rucksack load:

- *Make quite sure there's nothing there left over from a previous expedition*
- *Make use of all the pockets and compartments on your rucksack – you may not even realise they're there*
- *Pack lighter clothes for evening wear*
- *See if it's practicable for any equipment/clothes etc. to be sent on to you during the walk – with you sending 'used' equipment home at the same time*
- *Consider whether you can do without any reading books, especially hardbacks – many hotels and B & Bs are well stocked with reading material*
- *Consider what might be able to fit into the pockets of your jacket or even round your neck, e.g. binoculars, map case*

Sod's Law dictates: It's always the one item you need the most that will inevitably find its way into the most inaccessible part of your rucksack.

Choosing your long-distance walk

The Ordnance Survey Explorer maps reveal a vast number of long-distance routes in Great Britain alone. The choice is bewildering, and they vary tremendously in length, difficulty quality of signposting and amount of literature available.

Long-distance routes can be subdivided as follows:

National Trails (England and Wales)

Official Long Distance Walking Routes (Scotland)

Other 'name' paths, well established and maintained

Less well established and maintained 'name' paths

And we also need to mention the small matter of LEJOG or JOGLE!

National Trails (England and Wales)

These are State funded and generally very well maintained and signed, using the distinctive acorn logo. Every trail has a path manager who keeps in contact with the authorities that have funding and manpower available to deal with issues relating to that trail. Some of the trails have 'path associations' which issue publications and information and offer certificates or badges for successful completion. The course of every National Trail is clearly shown on the OS Explorer map. Though signage is generally good, navigational skills will still be required; no National Trail can realistically be walked on signage alone.

These are the National Trails, from shortest to longest: (ATTC – Average Time To Complete)

Yorkshire Wolds Way (79 miles/126 km, Hessle to Filey) – an undulating walk through unspoilt chalk uplands, characterised by steep dry valleys and lush pasture. Moderately difficult. ATTC 6 days

Hadrian's Wall Path (84 miles/134 km, Wallsend to Bowness-on-Solway) – a walk beside one of the most ancient man-made features in Britain through often stunning countryside. Strenuous in places. ATTC 7 days

Ridgeway (86 miles/138 km, Overton Hill to Ivinghoe Beacon) – a journey along ancient downland tracks through Wiltshire and Berkshire then a wider variety of landscapes in the Chiltern Hills. Easy. ATTC 6 days

Peddars Way and Norfolk Coast Path (95 miles/153 km, Knettishall Heath to Cromer) – a stretch of old Roman road through Breckland and level Norfolk countryside then gentle coastal scenery. Easy. ATTC 7 days

South Downs Way (96-99 miles/155-160 km, Winchester to Eastbourne) – a well-defined route along the chalk ridges of the South Downs, with spectacular views to the Weald and the sea. Moderately difficult. ATTC 8 days

Cotswold Way (102 miles/163 km, Bath to Chipping Campden) – an up and down journey along the Cotswold escarpment, glorious views, beautiful villages and small towns. Moderately difficult. ATTC 8 days

Cleveland Way (108 miles/172 km, Helmsley to Filey) – a traverse of the fringes of the North York Moors followed by a walk along some of the most spectacular coastal scenery in Eastern England. Strenuous. ATTC 8 days

- North Downs Way (125–130 miles/200–208 km, Farnham to Dover) – a walk along the escarpment of the North Downs through Surrey and Kent with fine views to the Weald and north towards London. Moderately difficult. ATTC 11 days

- Pennine Bridleway (still in construction: 130 miles/208 km so far, projected 350 miles/560 km, Middleton Top to Byrness) – a traverse of the Pennines on gentler paths, suitable for riders, cyclists and walkers. Moderately difficult. ATTC 21 days when complete.

- Glyndwr's Way (134 miles/214 km, Knighton to Welshpool) – an often rugged tramp through the heart of the remote mid-Wales countryside in the steps of Owain Glyndwr. Strenuous. ATTC 9 days.

- Pembrokeshire Coast Path (177 miles/283 km, St Dogmaels to Amroth) – a walk along the often uneven but spectacular coastline of south-west Wales, now a National Park. Strenuous. ATTC 14 days. NOTE: The whole route has been subsumed into the Wales Coast Path (see below)

- Offa's Dyke Path (178 miles/284 km, Sedbury to Prestatyn) – a superbly varied coast to coast walk following the England-Wales border based on the eighth century Offa's Dyke earthwork. Strenuous in places. ATTC 12 days

- Thames Path (185 miles/296 km, Source to Thames Barrier) – following the River Thames for almost all of its length, from tranquil unspoilt watermeadows to the bustling heart of London. Easy. ATTC 13 days

- Pennine Way (260 miles/320 km, Edale to Kirk Yetholm) – the father of all the National Trails, the first to open; a very demanding walk through the Dark Peak, Yorkshire Dales and up into the Cheviots. Severe. ATTC 19 days

- South West Coast Path (630 miles/1,008 km, Minehead to Poole) – our longest National Trail, following the stunning coastal/cliff scenery of Somerset, Devon, Cornwall and Dorset. Strenuous, severe in places. ATTC 7 week

Official Long-Distance Routes (Scotland)

These are maintained and funded in similar ways to National Trails, using the thistle as a waymark. Again, the course of each is clearly shown on the Explorer map. In the same way as National Trails, though signage is generally good, navigational skills are required to avoid losing the route. These are the Scottish official long-distance routes:

Great Glen Way (73 miles/117 km, Fort William to Inverness) – a superbly waymarked walk along the Great Glen in the Scottish Highlands, mostly beside lochs and the Caledonian Canal. Easy. ATTC 6 days

Speyside Way (80 miles/128 km, Buckie to Aviemore) – a delightful walk through the whisky centre of Great Britain. Easy. ATTC 6 days

West Highland Way (93 miles/149 km, Milngavie to Fort William) – a walk through fine Scottish Highland scenery using well-established paths and tracks. Strenuous in places. ATTC 7 days

Southern Upland Way (212 miles/340 km, Portpatrick to Cockburnspath) – a coast to coast walk across high level and often very remote terrain of southern Scotland. Strenuous. ATTC 13 days

Other named paths, well established and maintained

There are a huge number of such paths in Great Britain. They appear on Explorer maps, and in guidebooks, and can be found on the Internet. Cicerone publish a complete directory (see Appendix). Many could become National Trails in the future. Among the best known are:

The Dales Way – a 95 mile (152 km) walk from Leeds to Windermere, again passing through the Yorkshire Dales, over the Pennines and into the Lake District.

The London Loop – a 150 mile (241 km) walk, a sort of M25 for walkers but with fewer traffic cones and much prettier countryside, encircling the capital; and its younger brother the Capital Ring, a 78 mile (125 km) circular walk round Inner London.

Coast to Coast – a 192 mile (307 km) walk devised by Alfred Wainwright from St Bees on the west coast of England to Robin Hood's Bay on the east coast. It is more popular than many National Trails, passing as it does through the Lake District, Yorkshire Dales and North York Moors.

The Monarch's Way – a 615 mile (984 km) stroll from Powick Bridge in Worcestershire to Shoreham-by-Sea in West Sussex based on the route taken by King Charles II in fleeing Parliamentary forces.

…and, most recently of all, The Wales Coast Path – an 870 mile (1,392 km) walk round the entire coastline of Wales, from Chepstow in the south to Queensferry in the north, incorporating stunning coastal scenery which includes the whole of the Pembrokeshire Coast Path National Trail.

But these are just the tip of the iceberg – there are masses more.

Did you know that...
In the film Trainspotting, three of the characters go on a 'healthy hike' to Rannoch Moor which is part of the West Highland Way.

Top tip: If you've a serious interest in long-distance walking why not join the LDWA (Long-Distance Walkers' Association). It is intended for 'people with the common interest of walking long distances in rural, mountain or moorland areas'. At the time of writing there are forty-five local groups. It's a great way to meet like-minded people and obtain/exchange advice and form further walking friendships.

Less well established and maintained named paths

In theory it's possible for any individual or walking group, with co-operation from the authorities responsible for maintaining path signage, to establish their own 'name' path, using existing rights of way, and publicise it. With the help of social media you could even create and publicise your own long-distance walk!

Ideas for your own long-distance walk might include:

- A walk round the boundary of your county
- A walk linking every castle of your county
- A walk linking two or more cathedrals
- A walk linking two or more villages or towns of the same name
- A walk beside the longest-flowing river in your county (however far it goes – but remember, the Thames has already been done!)
- A walk linking monastic sites of the same foundation (Tony Hewitt of Cheadle, Cheshire, has devised an 'Augustinian Way' linking thirty-five monastic sites of Augustinian foundation, 1,140 miles/1,824 km in length from Pegwell Bay in Kent to Silloth Bay in Cumbria)
- A walk linking two extremes in Britain – the longest coast-to-coast, the longest line of latitude walk, etc. (Tony Hewitt has also devised walks around these themes)

LEJOG or JOGLE

The walk from Land's End to John o'Groats (LEJOG) or the other way round (JOGLE) – or simply 'end to end' – is not an official long-distance walk. Although it was first undertaken in the nineteenth century, it was in 1960 that this walk first really caught the public imagination when Billy Butlin – better known for his holiday camp – organised a challenge walk from 'end to end' with 138 finishers out of 715 starters. Since then, despite the lack of a waymarked route, it's an ambition for many walkers and a great means of raising money for charity.

How to do LEJOG

By road – it's reckoned that the shortest distance by road is around 814 miles (1,302 km) *but* this does include sections of motorway where walking is prohibited.

Conversely, seeking to avoid *all* roads as John Hillaby did (see chapter 6 below).

Using National Trails or other long-distance routes (a popular 'menu' is sections of South West Coast Path, Offa's Dyke Path, Pennine Way, West Highland Way and Great Glen Way) and the most direct convenient public footpath links between these sections.

Following the coastline all the way as John Merrill did (see chapter 6 below).

All the advice in relation to long-distance walking applies to an 'end to end' walk but two additional aspects need to be considered. To the mileage 'on the ground' needs to be added the numerous additional miles required to access accommodation and sustenance – you can't possibly carry all the food you'll need en route. Also consider whether you start at Land's End – with the advantage of the prevailing wind on your back – or at John o'Groats – with the psychological plus of it appearing to be downhill all the way.

But despite the logistics involved, to many who have discovered the joy of walking, conquest of the 'end to end' trail – a complete traverse of Great Britain – is their greatest achievement.

> **Did you know that...**
> The youngest person ever to walk from Land's End to John o'Groats is Joe Lambert, at the age of 9, back in 1993. It took him 40 days.

Long-distance walking overseas

> 'To see a world in a grain of sand,
> And a heaven in a wild flower;
> Hold infinity in the palm of your hand
> And eternity in an hour'
>
> WILLIAM BLAKE

While in Great Britain we are blessed with an astonishing variety of landscapes, we don't have the 'extremes' that other countries do, and which offer even richer and more challenging opportunities for the long-distance walker.

If you thought the above walks were challenging, here's our list of ten contenders for the top long-distance walking experiences around the world. Once you've become accustomed to wild *and* long-distance walking in Great Britain, why not try one – or more?

West Coast Trail – a 75 mile (120 km) trail in the Pacific Rim National Park, from Bamfield to Port Renfrew in Canada. There's a great diversity of scenery including waterfalls, forests and beaches, and wild animals including bears, wolves, sealions and cougars.

Inca Trail – regarded as the 'number 1' hiking trail in the world, there's actually a choice of trails, the most popular of which is the 'classic' going from Cuzco and leading to Machu Picchu, with mountains, rivers, lakes on your way as well as relics of the Incan civilisation. This trail is so popular that only 500 people are allowed on it per day. Distances vary depending on which of the Inca trails you opt for, but, for example, a four day walk covers roughly 28 miles (45 km) which tells you how tough the terrain is.

Monte Fitz Roy – located in Los Glaciares National Park in the Patagonia region of South America, a trail of around 40 miles (64 km) past lakes, mountains and glaciers.

The Laugevegur - a famous 34 miles (55 km) trekking route in south west Iceland taking typically up to four days, featuring hot springs, a glacial valley, and spectacular mountains and river crossings.

Tour du Mont Blanc - this goes round the Mont Blanc Massif in the Alps passing through France, Italy and Switzerland and is about 106 miles (170 km) long. There's 6 miles' worth of ascent and seven valleys to negotiate, but there are options for more challenging or easier routes within the whole.

El Camino de Santiago - one of the most important Christian pilgrimage routes during medieval times, there is in fact a choice of routes, most starting in France and all converging on Santiago di Compostela in Spain, supposedly the burial place of St James. It was declared the first European Cultural Route by the Council of Europe in 1987 and it's been named a UNESCO World Heritage Site. One popular route is from Roncesvalles to Santiago via Leon, 500 miles (800 km) and another, shorter one, is from Porto to Santiago via the Central Portuguese Way (227 km).

Annapurna Circuit – a trail varying between 100 and 145 miles (160 and 230 km) in Nepal and the Himalayas travelling through subtropical valleys, the deepest gorge in the world, Buddhist villages and Hindu holy sites.

John Muir Trail – a 215 mile (346 km) journey, named after a naturalist and advocate of wilderness preservation in the USA; it's a western USA trail from Yosemite National Park to Mount Whitney, the highest peak in the continental US, via forests, glaciers, mountains and lakes.

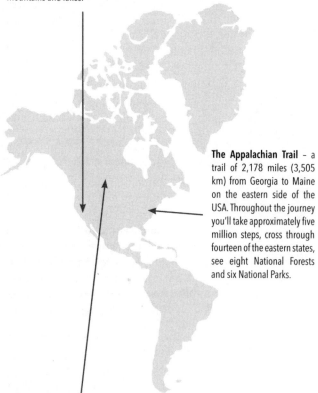

The Appalachian Trail – a trail of 2,178 miles (3,505 km) from Georgia to Maine on the eastern side of the USA. Throughout the journey you'll take approximately five million steps, cross through fourteen of the eastern states, see eight National Forests and six National Parks.

Which leaves just one more to mention – saving the longest till last…

Trans-Canada Trail – the world's longest network of recreational trails which when fully connected will stretch just over 14,000 miles (23,000 km) from the Atlantic to the Pacific to the Arctic oceans. It is 73 per cent complete and at the time of writing, more than 10,000 miles (16,000 km) is in use.

And you thought the South West Coast Path was long!

Did you know that...
A film based on the El Camino route was released in 2010. Called The Way, it was directed by Emilio Esteves and featured his real-life father Martin Sheen. Sheen stars as an American doctor who backpacks the route in memory of his son who died while walking it, and in doing so rediscovers his sense of identity and reconnects with the son he lost. Although the powerful and moving principal theme of this film is the desire of a father to connect with his deceased son through the pilgrimage journey, it is a hugely enjoyable and enriching film to watch by reason of the diversity of characters and stunning Basque scenery, culminating in the glorious images of Santiago itself, complemented by atmospheric and often haunting music. Anyone watching the film will be tempted to try the Camino for themselves.

CHAPTER 6

FAMOUS AND REMARKABLE WALKERS

*'It was then well past one o'clock and I had thirty miles
to walk, with only four hours of daylight left.'*
JOHN MERRILL, *TURN RIGHT AT LAND'S END*

Here we identify some of the most distinguished and colourful personalities in the world of walking – starting with three men and one woman who have walked round the world, and ending with one prolific walker who achieved immortality through his written work.

Dumitru Dan

Dan is believed to be the first man to have walked round the world. In 1908 the Touring Club De France announced a contest for walking round the world, with a prize of 100,000 francs. Dumitru Dan, a Romanian, was a student in Paris at the time, and decided to take up the challenge with three fellow Romanian students. In 1910, wearing native dress and walking in sandals, they set off with their dog Harap. All three of Dan's companions died en route; one through opium poison in India in 1911, one from a mountain accident in China in 1913, and one as a result of gangrene when crossing the USA. Dan then had to put his adventure on hold due to the outbreak of World War One but finally completed it in 1923 – although the actual value of his prize had diminished massively (to less than a tenth of what it had been in 1910).

Factfile

Dan…
- … wore out 497 pairs of shoes
- … crossed 5 continents and 3 oceans
- … visited 76 countries and over 1,500 cities
- … made it into the Guinness Book of Records and after his death in 1979 he was buried in a Heroes' Cemetery

Dave Kunst

Kunst, an American, was the first person whose circumnavigation of the world was verified. He started in Waseca, Minnesota in June 1970 and finished in October 1974. He began the journey with his brother John and a mule named Willie Makeit. All went well initially; they walked to New York and, leaving the mule there, flew to Portugal (acquiring a second mule). They then crossed Europe and continued on into Afghanistan where they were attacked by bandits and John was killed. Dave survived the attack but was injured. After a four month lay-off, he continued with another brother, Pete. Denied access to the USSR they flew from India to Australia. Pete returned but Dave continued, with a third mule. This mule died but a Perth schoolteacher agreed to transport Dave's supplies by car. At length Kunst completed his journey, returned to Australia and married the schoolteacher. Both are still alive and together today.

Factfile

Kunst...
- ... walked 20 million steps
- ... wore out 21 pairs of shoes
- ... crossed four continents and thirteen countries
- ... had a dog house built in his wagon so he could transport one of their canine companions
- ... walked through the Khyber Pass with a Pakistani tribal prince

Jean Béliveau

In 2011, the Canadian Béliveau completed the longest recorded walk around the world, measured at 47,000 miles (75,000 km), and the longest uninterrupted walk in human history. His trek began on his forty-fifth birthday in August 2000, the result, he says, of a mid-life crisis, and ended eleven years later. He stayed with 1,600 different families during his walk and visited 64 countries. Among his most vivid memories were eating snake in China and insects in Africa, being escorted by armed soldiers in the Philippines, a close encounter with a puma in a South American desert, and being kidnapped by escaped murderers.

Factfile

- *The reason for his marathon walk was to draw attention to child victims of violence, which coincided with a United Nations initiative on this issue*
- *He said the hardest part of the planning was telling his wife what he was going to do*
- *He carried his equipment in a 3-wheeled 'stroller'*
- *He wore out 49 pairs of shoes*
- *On his walk he met four Nobel Peace Prize winners including Nelson Mandela who told him 'the world needs people like you.'*

Ffyona Campbell

Born in 1967, Campbell was the first woman to walk round the world (albeit not continuously), covering 20,000 miles (32,000 km) over eleven years, raising £180,000 for charity.

After leaving school at sixteen, she walked from John o'Groats to Land's End, completing the journey in forty-nine days; at that time she was the youngest person to have done this. At eighteen she crossed the USA on foot from New York to Los Angeles, a distance of some 3,500 miles (5,600 km). Owing to illness she was unable to keep up the very demanding schedule she set for herself and in order to avoid letting anyone down she on three occasions accepted a lift from her back-up driver to make up time.

Determined to show she could complete a long-distance trek without missing any miles, at twenty-one she walked 3,200 miles (5,120 km) across Australia, covering some 50 miles a day with no missed sections; her adventures are described in her book *Feet of Clay*. Then starting in April 1991 in Cape Town she walked the entire length of Africa covering over 9,900 miles (16,000 km) and ending at Tangier in Morocco in September 1993. During her journey she had to be evacuated by the French Foreign Legion from Zaire owing to an uprising, but was able to return and continue; she then had to do an extra 2,500 miles (4,000 km) round a war zone! Her journey is described in her book *On Foot Through Africa*. Then in April 1994 she walked right through Europe, starting at Algeciras in Spain and on returning to Britain, walking all the way up to John o'Groats. Not content with all that, she returned to the USA and this time managed to cross the continent without any lifts. This journey is described in her book *The Whole Story*.

Factfile

- *Campbell raised money for charity by selling advertising space on her forehead*
- *Inspired by hunter-gatherers she met on her walk, she lived among the Aborigines for three months and has since taught people in Britain to be hunter-gatherers*
- *Born into a Naval family, she attended fifteen schools and as a child moved home twenty-four times*

'I sank down under the shower and thought: this is real! I'd imagined it so often. It was absolute, indescribable luxury.'

ON FOOT THROUGH AFRICA

'I walked on across flat, open plains of succulent green shrubs and yellow grass, towards a far distant horizon.'

ON FOOT THROUGH AFRICA

John Hillaby

A British travel writer who was born in 1917 and died in 1996, Hillaby is remarkable for his quest to walk from Land's End to John o'Groats without using any roads at all. Although that was his avowed intention, he found it impossible because too many paths had become overgrown, enclosed, ploughed up or obstructed. The walk is described in his book *Journey Through Britain*, published in 1968 and arguably the best written account of the 'end to end' walk ever to have appeared in print.

> 'Walking is intimate: it releases something unknown in any other form of travel.'
>
> JOURNEY THROUGH BRITAIN

> 'Could it be that cartographers were in league with the woodsmen in an effort to confound incursionists?'
>
> JOURNEY THROUGH BRITAIN

Factfile

- *Hillaby also undertook a 1,000 mile (1,600 km) walk with a camel train through northern Kenya to Lake Turkana, which he described in his book* Journey To The Jade Sea, *published in 1964*
- *He also accomplished a walk across Europe, recounted in his book* Journey Through Europe *published in 1972*
- *Both these journeys were undertaken alone but in 1981 he married Kathleen Burton who also loved walking and she featured in his later books as his walking companion*

Did you know that...
Although Land's End is the extreme south-westerly point of Great Britain the most southerly point is Lizard Point, and although John o' Groats is the commonly acknowledged extreme northern point of mainland Scotland the actual northernmost point is at nearby Dunnet Head.

John Merrill

Born in London on 19 August 1943, he could be described as a professional marathon walker, active in undertaking very long walks and describing routes for readers to follow. He also lectures extensively on the subject. His walks include:

Hebridean Journey – 1,003 miles (1,614 km)
Parkland Journey – 2,043 miles (3,288 km)
Land's End to John o'Groats – 1,608 miles (2,588 km)
Across the USA coast to coast – 4,226 miles (6,801 km) in 178 days
Appalachian Trail – just under 2,200 miles (3,500 km)
Pacific Crest Trail – 2,700 miles (4,300 km)
Continental Divide – 4,500 miles (7,200 km)
Le Puy to Santiago di Compostela – 1,100 miles (1,760 km)

Factfile

- *Merrill calculates he's walked over 206,000 miles (329,600 km) between 1969 and 2013*
- *His walking has raised over £750,000 for charity*
- *He's author of well over 300 walking guides;*
- *He never carries water (don't try this at home!);*
- *He says the limit of endurance is 200 miles (320 km) a week;*
- *He's worn out 118 pairs of boots, over 1,000 pairs of socks and 43 rucksacks;*
- *He's also an ordained Minister*

However, perhaps his greatest claim to fame is that he became the first person to walk the entire coastline of Great Britain on an almost-continuous expedition between January and November 1978. It wasn't quite continuous in that he suffered a foot fracture and had to rest for a month or so during the walk. The total mileage covered was 6,824 (10,982 km). Apart from his injury break he had only one – unscheduled – rest day (caused by bad weather) and covered the entire distance on foot, only using vehicles to convey him from his finishing point on any given day and return him back to that same point the next day. Not satisfied with walking the coastline, he incorporated climbs of Snowdon, Scafell Pike and Ben Nevis into his itinerary. He averaged 26 miles (42 km) a day with 50–60 lb (22–27kg) of equipment; on 22 October 1978, he walked from King's Lynn to Holkham, a distance of 39 miles (62.5 km). His extraordinary feat was chronicled in his book *Turn Right at Land's End*. Some extracts:

'I shuddered inside as the enormity of what I had achieved so far became clear.'

'With almost 2,300 miles behind me I was beginning to feel very fit.'

'To have found a wife on the walk was a bonus I had definitely not expected.'

George Meegan

Meegan is famous for his unbroken walk of the entire Western hemisphere, from the southern tip of South America to the northernmost part of Alaska, a distance of 19,019 miles (30,608 km). Starting in 1977 and ending in 1983, unbroken and unaided by any transport, the walk was:

The first journey on foot crossing South and Central America

The first journey on foot crossing Latin America

The first journey on foot crossing from the Tropic of Capricon via the Equator to the Tropic of Cancer

The first journey on foot between the Equator and the Arctic Circle

The first journey on foot to connect the Southern, Atlantic, Pacific and Arctic Oceans

It was also the most degrees of latitude ever covered on foot

---

Factfile

- *Meegan estimates he took 31 million steps*
- *He visited 14 countries*
- *He was briefly imprisoned as a vagrant in Argentina*
- *In 2010 he stood as an independent parliamentary candidate in the Gillingham & Rainham constituency – and came last*
- *At the end of his walk Meegan said: 'I've just lost my best friend – I've run out of road.'*

Shaul Ladany and some other fast walkers

Racewalking first appeared in the modern Olympics in 1904 as a half-mile walk in the then equivalent of the decathlon. In 1908, standalone 1,500 m (1,650 yds) and 3,000 m (3,300 yds) race walks were added, but modern Olympic events are the 20 km (12.4 miles) race walk for men and women, and 50 km (31 miles) race walk for men only. However there are longer races in other events including one of 50 miles (80 km).

 The record for the 50 mile (80 km) race walk is held by the Israeli Shaul Ladany who accomplished the race in 7 hours, 23 minutes and 50 seconds in New Jersey in 1972.

 The record for the 12.4 mile (20 km) race walk is held by Vladimir Kanaykin of Russia who accomplished the race in 1 hour 17 minutes and 16 seconds in Saransk in September 2007.

 The women's record for the same distance is held by Olimpiada Ivanova of Russia who accomplished the race in 1 hour 24 minutes and 50 seconds in Adler in March 2001.

 The record for the 31 mile (50 km) race walk is held by Denis Nizhegorodov of Russia who accomplished the race in 3 hours 34 minutes and 14 seconds in Cheboksary in May 2008.

Walkers who just kept going

According to *Guinness World Records*, the greatest distance walked in 24 hours is 142 miles 440 yards (227 km) by the American Jesse Castaneda at Albuquerque, New Mexico, on 18/19 September 1976.

Georges Holtyzer of Belgium walked 418.49 miles (673 km) in 6 days, 10 hours and 58 minutes between July 19 and July 26 1986.

In 2004, David Macatinney and Russell Fowler walked non-stop (no sleep, no rest) for 154 hours and 5 minutes inside Western Australia's Fremantle Prison heritage site.

But we save the best walker till last......

Alfred Wainwright

Although Wainwright never matched the aggregate distances or speeds achieved by the above, he is arguably the most famous and best-loved British walker of all, not simply because of his own achievements but because of his guidebooks which have inspired millions of people to enjoy the same landscapes and get the same pleasure out of walking as he did.

Alfred Wainwright was born in Blackburn, Lancashire on 17 January 1907 and started work as an office boy in the town's borough engineers department, subsequently developing his career with Blackburn Borough Council, but even at a young age he walked a good deal and showed a great interest in cartography. He travelled to the Lake District for the first time in 1930 and so loved the area that he decided to move there, taking a job at the Kendal Borough Treasurers Office where he remained until he retired in 1967. His love affair with the Lake District stayed with him for life.

Wainwright began work on his first *Pictorial Guide To The Lakeland Fells* in 1952 and completed the seventh volume 13 years later (though in 1974 he completed a guide to the outlying Lakeland fells). He would use weekends and holidays for his field work and spend each evening on the writing and drawing, averaging a page a day. Initially he published his books privately but from 1963 they were published by the Westmorland Gazette. Later Michael Joseph and then (and still at the time of writing) Frances Lincoln took over publication. The guides were unique in many respects. They were all hand drawn with no use of computer; the illustrations were actually more useful than maps in including helpful features such as gates, stiles, sheepfolds etc. to aid navigation, and the accompanying text showed a great empathy for the walker, as if he knew exactly how the walker would be feeling and what he would be experiencing at any given point in a walk. His walk descriptions are crammed with wisdom, of which some examples are given below.

Not content with guides to the Lake District, Wainwright prepared a guide to the Pennine Way - his *Pennine Way Companion*, duly updated, is still arguably the best of all the Pennine Way guides available - and in 1972 he devised his own Coast to Coast Walk (see p.127). Although this still, remarkably, lacks any 'official' status at all, it is one of the most popular walking routes in Great Britain and was once voted the second best walk in the world! He went on to produce a large number of books and television programmes, and since his death there have been numerous programmes about him and his walks. He was married twice; he divorced his first wife Ruth and in 1970 married Betty, an enthusiastic walker to whom he was devoted for the rest of his life. He died in 1991. Meanwhile his original pictorial guides have continued to sell in huge numbers; to date they've sold more than 2 million copies.

Factfile

- The 214 Lakeland fells described in his Pictorial Guides *have become known as Wainwrights and visiting them all is a common form of 'peak bagging' with well over 400 people having done the lot, one as young as five years of age*
- Most of the profits from his books went to animal welfare charities
- His Pennine Way Companion *describes the walk backwards, the route description beginning towards the end of the book and ending towards the start*
- He wrote in the region of sixty books, provided material for a dozen more, and around twenty books have been written about him and his work

The wisdom of Alfred Wainwright

'Always, at Keld, there is the music of the water.'
PENNINE WAY COMPANION

'One should always have a definite objective, in a walk as in life.'
A COAST TO COAST WALK

'The best form of walking is fell walking and the best part of fell walking is ridge walking.'
A COAST TO COAST WALK

There ought to be a word for it...

Disappointment that the rapport you established with the attractive stranger at the top of Ben Nevis isn't replicated when you next meet at the Tesco in-store cafe in Reading

Life-affirming and hugely walk-enhancing gastronomic experience in en route pub or restaurant such as consumption of enormous bowlful of syrup sponge pudding with lashings of custard

Descriptive of hypnotic state in which new convert to the joys of walking spends entire evenings checking out comparison websites for the best value boot polish

Virtuous feeling experienced by walker having spent his Sunday evening re-waterproofing his walking jacket, gelling his walking boots and correctly pairing up freshly laundered walking socks

Obsessive walker's pursuit of unlikely and somewhat offbeat objective e.g. the most north-westerly point of each county in Great Britain or exploration on foot of all places in Great Britain beginning with the letter Q

Feeling of deflation you get when having completed what you regarded as a fierce climb and descent, you read a book about the same walk describing the climb as 'one which you could comfortably take your granny up after your second helping of Christmas pudding'

Regrettable sense of self-satisfaction on reaching hilltop in beautifully clear conditions then descending from it and meeting other walkers heading towards it just as it becomes totally enveloped in mist

Sensation of arriving ravenously hungry at pub or cafe at 2.16 p.m. in the course of a long walk, only to be told that 'we stop serving food at 2.15 p.m.'

Having placed everything you have decided to take with you on your walking holiday in your rucksack and zipped it up with extreme difficulty, infuriatingly spotting small item you're wanting to take but find is still sitting on the carpet in your front room

The act of breaking off a chunk of chocolate-coated Kendal Mint Cake onto open page of Wainwright guide on a cloudless golden autumn morning on a Lakeland mountainside with nobody else about and thinking it can't get any better than this

CONCLUSION

Our exploration of the joy of walking is almost over. You've learned of the many reasons why it's great to walk. You've learned how many amazing walking opportunities exist both on your own doorstep and right across Great Britain and abroad. And you'll have been inspired by the many achievements of many amazing walkers. We wish you all the best as you embark on your own journeys of exploration and wonder! Happy walking.

FURTHER READING AND INFORMATION

These days getting information on all aspects of walking is very easy thanks to the Internet. Googling pretty much any name, place, subject or article mentioned above will open up literally thousands of websites and web entries. It would be pointless to list all the websites I use to get information from; there are just too many.

If Google is all too technical for you, your best bet is your local public library or, for information about walks in the locality, your nearest tourist information office.

I do recommend a number of books, some of which sadly are out of print but which you may be able to get from the library, a second-hand bookseller or on eBay!

Ffyona Campbell – *On Foot Through Africa* (Orion, 1994)
Campbell's account of her astonishing, courageous and inspiring African journey, against all the odds, from Cape Town to Tangier.

John Merrill – *Turn Right at Land's End* (Oxford Illustrated Press, 1980)
Merrill's account, in diary form, of his epic coast walk in 1978.

John Hillaby – *Journey Through Britain* (Constable, 1968)

Arguably the definitive account of the end-to-end walk, beautifully written.

Alfred Wainwright – *Pictorial Guide to Lakeland Fells* (Frances Lincoln, various)

Quite simply, the best walking guidebooks ever written.

Alfred Wainwright – *Pennine Way Companion* (Westmorland Gazette, 1968)

Still regarded as the definitive work on the subject.

Alfred Wainwright – *A Coast To Coast Walk* (Westmorland Gazette, 1973)
Much revised since but a true labour of love.

H. D. Westacott – *The Walker's Handbook* (Penguin, 1978)
Full of very practical advice, much of it still holding good 35 years on.

Gavin Pretor-Pinney – *The Cloudspotter's Guide* (Sceptre, 2007)
By the chairman and founder member of the Cloud Appreciation Society; looking up will never be the same again.

Paddy Dillon – *The National Trails* (Cicerone, 2007)

An at-a-glance guide to Britain's primary long-distance routes, superbly illustrated.

The Trailwalkers' Handbook (Cicerone, 2010)

A guide to almost every named path in Britain – enough walking for several lifetimes.

Alan Plowright – *Plowright Follows Wainwright* (Michael Joseph, 1995)

An inspiring, very readable and amusing account of a Yorkshireman's discovery of the joy of walking.

Sinclair McKay – *Ramble On* (Fourth Estate, 2012)

An excellent recent social history of walking for pleasure.

David Bathurst – *Walking the County High Points of England* (Summersdale, 2012)

A guide to scaling every county summit, varying hugely in difficulty and terrain.

If you're interested in finding out more about our books,
find us on Facebook at **Summersdale Publishers** and follow us
on Twitter at **@Summersdale**.

www.summersdale.com